# Think Again;
## *Ways to Dismantle Lousy Leadership*

## Other Books By Karl Bimshas

"So, I've Been Thinking; *Seemingly Random Thoughts on Leadership*"

"So, I've Been Thinking Some More; *Reflections on Leadership*"

"How to Fix Your Whine at Work"

"Quick Ways to Be a Good Leader"

"Don't Be the A-Hole on The Team"

"Leaders Don't Shrug; *Advice for Busy Professionals*"

"GO GET IT!; *Your Guide to Finding Purpose, Setting Goals and Maintaining Success*,"

"Pushing Back the Ocean; *Tide Turning Leadership Lessons*,"

"How to Stay When You Want to Quit; *Re-scripting your life from whiner to winner*,"

"Disposable Journal; *Write it out and let it go*,"

"Write Advice; *Inspirations, tips, and thoughts for Leaders and Artists*."

"Perspectives, *A 30 Day Journal to View Your World Differently*"

# Think Again;
## *Ways to Dismantle Lousy Leadership*

Karl Bimshas

**Bim**Media

*San Diego, California*

Copyright © 2018 Karl Bimshas

*All rights reserved. All rights reserved. This publication or any portion thereof may not be reproduced, or used in and manner whatsoever without the express written permission of the publisher except for the use of brief quotations in a book review or scholarly journal.*

*First Printing 2018*
*Karl Bimshas Consulting*
*7676 Hazard Center Drive, Suite 500*
*San Diego, CA 92108*

*www.KarlBimshasConsulting.com*

*Photo credit: Jonas Bimshas*

ISBN: 9781726836913

# DEDICATION

*This book is for the countless, nameless, faceless people who intuitively know the difference between "right" and "wrong" and bravely face injustice and frankly, the stupidity that is often found in lousy leaders. They do not seek fame, power, or accolades. They, like me, only want to upgrade the level of leadership in the world, and to take direction from people who manage better and lead well.*

# TABLE OF CONTENTS

| | |
|---|---|
| INTRODUCTION | 11 |
| SIMPLE RULE | 13 |
| HOW MUCH DO YOU PAY IN LOUSY LEADER TAX? | 14 |
| START TO LEAD – DARE TO GIVE A DAMN | 17 |
| LEADERSHIP CAN BE LONELY | 18 |
| FRIENDS DON'T LET FRIENDS BECOME LOUSY LEADERS | 19 |
| IS YOUR LEADERSHIP WORKING? | 20 |
| FALLING PREY TO LOUSY LEADERSHIP | 21 |
| BE OUTSPOKEN | 23 |
| REJECTING LEADERSHIP | 25 |
| TWO LOUSY LEADERS | 26 |
| DON'T BE AFRAID TO LEAD | 27 |
| EMPATHY AND CURIOSITY | 28 |
| MUST BE PRESENT TO WIN | 29 |
| PASSION ON A PEDESTAL | 30 |
| NEW DAY | 31 |
| DON'T JUST SIT THERE. THINK ABOUT IT. | 32 |
| BE A BETTER GATEKEEPER | 33 |
| YOUR 90 DAY REVIEW | 34 |
| HARMONY OVER BALANCE | 35 |
| 13 MONTHS | 37 |
| VISCERAL LEADERSHIP | 39 |
| HOW DO YOU INVEST YOUR TIME OVER A LONG WEEKEND? | 40 |
| "LET ME FAIL" | 41 |
| HOW YOU BECOME SUCCESSFUL MATTERS | 43 |
| YOU'VE GOT THIS | 45 |
| ALONE, OR WITH YOUR FLOCK, SOAR | 46 |
| WHY? BECAUSE! | 47 |
| ENJOY LEADING OR DON'T LEAD | 48 |
| NO REFUGE FOR POOR LEADERS | 49 |
| WALK WITH PURPOSE, NOT CONFUSION | 50 |
| LEADERSHIP INGREDIENTS | 51 |
| YOU ALWAYS MAKE A DIFFERENCE | 52 |
| LEAD THE CHANGE OR LEAD THE SAME | 53 |
| BE THE BETTER OPTION | 55 |
| BE READY TO LEAD | 56 |
| SOMETHING MISSING? | 57 |
| MONDAY EXCITEMENT | 58 |
| LUCK AND GOOD FORTUNE | 59 |

| Are You Acting On Purpose? | 60 |
| --- | --- |
| How You Doin'? | 61 |
| Never Feel Lost | 62 |
| Fix It | 63 |
| Great Goal | 64 |
| You Don't Need Permission to Lead | 65 |
| Head and Heart in Leadership | 66 |
| Are You Bad for Business? | 67 |
| Don't Wait to be Empowered | 68 |
| Raise Your Standards | 69 |
| It Starts with Purpose | 70 |
| Five Reasons Why Some Executives Do Not Put Poor Performing Leaders on Corrective Action | 71 |
| Knowing Your Values | 73 |
| You Can Thank Your Lousy Boss | 74 |
| Daily Focus | 76 |
| How's Your Leadership-Life Going? | 77 |
| Lousy Leadership Is Easy but Expensive | 79 |
| How Many Under Your Watch? | 81 |
| Leaders Ask | 83 |
| Poor Leadership Pisses Me Off | 84 |
| Moving Your Passion Toward Excellence | 86 |
| Hedge Less; Lead Better | 89 |
| Don't Retreat | 91 |
| Do Your Direct Reports Need Leadership Coaching? | 93 |
| Refuse Generational Labels; You'll Lead Better | 94 |
| Adapt Your Style | 97 |
| For Leaders who Cringe on Sundays | 98 |
| Don't Listen to Them; You're Fine | 99 |
| Writing Letters to Your Younger Self | 101 |
| Basketball Players, Filmmakers, and Nurses | 103 |
| How's Your Customer Love Life? | 105 |
| 4 Time Chunks for Better Performance | 106 |
| Are You an Authoritarian at Work? | 108 |
| Guard the Gate | 111 |
| Run an After Action Review for Your Year | 113 |
| Your Year Was Not Great | 116 |
| Decide with SPICE | 118 |
| Your Leadership Agenda | 120 |
| Remember Context | 122 |
| Focus Can Be Difficult | 123 |

| | |
|---|---|
| ORGANIZE YOUR THOUGHTS | 124 |
| DECIDE HOW YOU ARE GOING TO LEAD | 125 |
| DON'T IMITATE | 127 |
| LEADERSHIP MAINTENANCE | 128 |
| EXPECT THE BEST, PLAN FOR THE WORST | 130 |
| LOUSY LEADERSHIP IS SCARY | 131 |
| YOU GOOFED. NOW WHAT? | 133 |
| NO, YOUR CUSTOMERS DON'T ALL LOVE YOU | 135 |
| CULTIVATING SUCCESS | 137 |
| FRIENDS | 140 |
| INTEGRITY | 141 |
| FIND A WAY TO LAUGH | 142 |
| LOUSY LEADERS PISS ME OFF | 143 |
| GOOD LEADERS | 144 |
| ART AND SCIENCE | 145 |
| CHANGE THINGS | 146 |
| SMALL STEPS | 147 |
| MOTHER'S DAY | 148 |
| EVERY DAY IS BEAUTIFUL | 149 |
| PRICEY MISSION | 150 |
| BE A LEADER. NOT A PRIG. NOT A PRICK | 151 |
| DECIDE TO LEAD | 152 |
| STEP IT UP | 153 |
| CRISIS PROMOTION | 154 |
| ROARING ISN'T WHAT MAKES YOU A LEADER | 155 |
| WORDS MATTER | 156 |
| WHERE YOU DWELL | 157 |
| THE MYTH OF EASE | 158 |
| BETTER GOALS | 159 |
| USE YOUR VOICE | 160 |
| LISTEN | 161 |
| INDIFFERENCE DOES NOT INFLUENCE | 162 |
| RAISE YOUR EXPECTATIONS | 163 |
| IF YOU CANNOT LISTEN, YOU CANNOT LEAD | 164 |
| YOUR VALUES DRIVE YOUR BEHAVIOR | 165 |
| UNDER APPRECIATING | 166 |
| BONUS - 20 MAXIMS | 167 |
| FINAL THOUGHTS | 173 |
| ABOUT THE AUTHOR | 175 |

Karl Bimshas

# INTRODUCTION

It can feel like we are in the midst of a lousy leader epidemic. From laughable errors in judgment, illogical lapses in commonsense, to plots that are more sinister, it's easy to mock those in power. There's a better way. Step up and provide better leadership.

Imagine if you started to lead, instead of whining.

What could you accomplish if you dared to give a damn?

Live your values and act on purpose. It is the simplest, most straightforward way you can identify leadership in yourself and others.

If you want to manage better and lead well, this is where you start. No one can make you, and you cannot fake giving a damn.

Too many supposed leaders lack this attribute, and it is why they fail themselves, and those they claim to lead.

I stand for better leadership. People need to begin to recognize that positive leadership is everywhere. I'm committed to redefining how we look at effective leadership. It isn't haughty and lofty; it's selfless and accessible.

I'm not only interested in making better leaders for the world, I want to make the world full of better leaders.

The essays, thoughts, and musing in the following reflections on leadership can act as a guidebook on preventative care. It is a human trait to let the perks of leadership overshadow the purpose. This book is an attempt to keep leaders and soon to be leaders focused and performing with integrity, empathy, and humor.

Karl Bimshas

## *Simple Rule*

Ask yourself, "What would a lousy leader do?" Then, make damn sure you don't do that.

Success leaves clues, so too does failure. Pay attention to the lessons that surround you. Very few wake up in the morning determined to be a lousy leader, but through arrogance, dogma, lack of curiosity, or a moral compass that spins like a propeller, that's where they end up.

Defend yourself against this with lousy leader prevention. When you are faced with a dilemma, imagine what a lousy leader would do. Do the opposite!

It may not always be the exact opposite, but by examining your potential actions through the lens of a lousy leader, before committing to them, you will more likely choose the better path.

And remember to lighten up. Don't take everything so seriously. Things are neither bad nor good. It's your attitude that makes them so. Be professional. Be sincere. Tone down the theatrics. Good leaders project calmness and confidence, even if they temporarily lack both. Leaders laugh often because they know lessons with laughter last longer.

## *How Much Do You Pay in Lousy Leader Tax?*

Leaders play an important role in any organization. Great ones have a compound additive effect, which we frequently celebrate. Are those accolades overstated? If esteemed polls and studies are to be believed, we seldom crack the 30-35% range of fully engaged, productive, and capable leaders. Perhaps that percentage doesn't rise because organizations large and small have grown complacent with their intractable lousy leaders.

Lousy leaders most often lack the essential leadership abilities, which others have mislabeled as "soft skills." In truth, poor leaders often lack the "hard skills" required for their job too. Hard skills are the standard, industry-specific skill sets that by all accounts, are the price of admission. Nearly everyone in a given sector has these required skills to one degree or another, or they wouldn't be there.

The variance that keeps lousy leaders in power is their knowledge or their perceived knowledge. Years of experience do not always translate easily into years of competence, but often, we mistakenly think it does. There is also nefarious knowledge; knowing trade secrets and where the proverbial skeletons are hidden within the organization. Mix in ego, fear, and the worry of humiliation, and you suddenly understand why some weaker executives are hesitant to act.

Isn't the cost of inaction too high? For some, no, it is a bargain. However, for many, particularly small business owners, the price paid for lousy leadership is unknown. That's no way to manage a successful business, so let's attempt to codify the costs (or investments if you're happy with performance) in four categories.

1. Employee Turnover
2. Customer Defections
3. Drag on Productivity
4. Discretionary Nonsense

Run the following conservative calculations over the last twelve-month period for each of your leaders.

For Employee Turnover, estimate 20% of the annual salary for any employee that has voluntarily left the organization.

Calculate the number of Customer Defections under the leader's span of control. In other words, how many clients did the leader have 12 months ago versus today? Turn that number into a percentage and then multiply it by four. (e.g. A 5% Customer Defection Rate x 4 = 20%.) Subtract that adjusted percentage from your expected profit.

Calculate the leader's Operating Productivity by dividing the estimated revenue by the number of team members, (also considered the revenue per employee.) The estimated productivity drag of a lousy leader is 10% of the operating productivity.

Discretionary Nonsense is the total miscellaneous expenses you are accumulating to keep the lousy leader in a status quo position. This could be unusually large items on an expense report and any perks they have negotiated that others in the organization don't have, i.e., company car. Also include potential court expenses, attorney fees, and if you are the kind of organization that is paying settlements for non-work related activities, those would be lumped into this category. By the way, if the line items in this category are higher than any of the others, you have far more significant problems in your organizational culture than any one leader.

The total of all four categories is the "tax" you and your organization are paying to keep the lousy leader in their position.

If you are a small firm, the leader is new, and the expense is manageable, this might be an acceptable number for you short-term. If the return on investment in this leader is unacceptable, you will need to use your discretion as to where this money could be better spent. Perhaps in better leadership training, development and accountability; or maybe, if you can catch them before they leave, in the promotion of the capable leaders who are already in your midst but have been hidden from view.

Conversely, you can make these calculations positively. No turnover is, neutral, client acquisition is margin added, and there is an uplift to operating productivity. You would be well advised to share the wealth with these effective leaders; the odds are, they would reinvest in their team.

So, how much do you pay in lousy leader tax? Is it worth it, or would you prefer to expand your profit?

## *Take Leadership Seriously and Yourself Lightly*

Even self-leadership, which can be the most difficult, because of your varying levels of obstinance, procrastination, perfectionism, and self-confidence, requires a gentle, nudge.

Leadership is important. It can have positive or negative effects on teams, families, generations, and nations. It's no laughing matter — but you are. You are fallible, mistake-prone, occasionally pig-headed, and susceptible to flattery. You're human, which means you can laugh — and you should. Besides, if you take yourself too seriously, the laughter won't stop, it will just be behind your back.

Build your self-awareness. Grab a few leadership assessments, or check in with an accountability partner to see how you're doing. If you're leading, you're teaching, and remember, lessons with laughter last longer.

## *Start to Lead – Dare to Give a Damn*

Imagine if you started to lead, instead of whining.

What could you accomplish if you dared to give a damn?

Live your values and act on purpose. It is the simplest, most straightforward way you can identify leadership in yourself and others.

If you want to manage better and lead well, this is where you start. No one can make you, and you cannot fake giving a damn.

Too many supposed leaders lack this attribute, and it is why they fail themselves, and those they claim to lead.

I stand for better leadership. People need to begin to recognize that positive leadership is everywhere. I'm committed to redefining how we look at effective leadership. It isn't haughty and lofty, it's selfless and accessible.

I invite you to join me in declaring war against lousy leaders. There's no sign up sheet or coupon code required. It's a simple two-step process.
1. Say, "I'm in."
2. Start to give a damn.

I'm not only interested in making better leaders for the world, I want to make the world full of better leaders.

## *Leadership Can Be Lonely*

Did you know many busy leaders feel like an imposter because they are struggling with their self-leadership?

As a result, their confidence takes a hit, and they find themselves failing to speak up or advocate for better ideas.

They tuck away these daily mini-failures and still carry them because often they don't have an outlet to share their concerns or fresh approaches, free from fear of being labeled a whiner or a workaholic – if they are listened to at all.

You may have imagined what it would be like to feel genuinely confident in your leadership abilities, have your ideas heard, respected, and supported by others.

Well, you don't have to imagine anymore…

## *Friends Don't Let Friends Become Lousy Leaders*

Ever come across a friend or family member who was screwing up their leadership? It usually happens about 18 months into their role. By that time the honeymoon is over and they start clashing with employees and colleagues.

You might not notice it at first. They stopped talking about work as much lately, but something happened and they need to vent.

You listen as they complain about how people have become incompetent, aren't taking direction, and seem to have become stupid overnight. You know, it's *possible* those things may be true, and you want to be supportive, but … it sure does sound like they're whining.

They are likely under pressure, questioning themselves, feeling a lot of uncertainty, but are trying to hide it behind bravado. That's the wrong tactic and if they proceed, they risk becoming a lousy leader.

Friends don't let friends become lousy leaders. You have an opportunity to talk some sense into them. Don't squander the trust. Show them some tough love and encouragement. If you need help, reach out to us.

## *Is Your Leadership Working?*

Are you getting the results you want and need?

Do you have a high-performing team, or just a group of people who work together?

Are you energized or drained at the end (or the beginning) of each day?

Are you making progress and recognizing the efforts being made, or are you stagnating and blaming?

If you could have a strong leader on your team, would you pick you? Would your team?

Your leadership style, approach, attitude might not be very effective right now. What are you going to do to improve your leadership development and accountability?

## *Falling Prey to Lousy Leadership*

It starts with convenience and familiarity. The lousy leader is known to you; charming and fun to be around, or they may have helped you during tough times, so you feel indebted.

Soon, they want you to do special favors for them. They are acts you don't feel comfortable doing, but you quickly talk yourself into them because you do not want to cause disappointment. In a confounding mental game, you warp the "get out of your comfort zone" mantra, into betraying your values; a destructive choice that becomes easier with repetition.

Next, you also begin to betray old friendships, convinced that people are holding you back, unsupportive, or have an agenda. Caring about you is not a strong enough reason, because you are now surrounded by others who tell you that caring is a weakness that prevents you from making real money. Ironically, conversations with your new "friends" likely occur over bottomless early-afternoon drinks; their wisdom spewed between slurred speech and bursts of drunken laughter. You pick up the tab because you appreciate the insights and attention.

In time, you achieve a few financial successes, but it's not enough. You're in a hole, so it doesn't feel like progress. You are impatient instead of disciplined; your ambition morphs into greed. You are less flexible, more opportunistic. Everything. Ev-er-y-thing, is about making a buck or increasing your power.

Connections to your past dwindle until only one item remains. Like Citizen Kane's "Rosebud," you have a sole touchstone that reveals your true self; a piece of jewelry, a book, a beloved pet, or an old set of tools. Eventually, it too disappears, and you mourn, not for the loss of the item, for the loss of your inner goodness and the direction you could have taken but choose not to. It is at this hour that your transformation is complete. You fully embrace the ease and cowardliness of lousy leadership because you believe you are too far down the path and cannot return.

It is thought that the potential to save thousands of lives is what motivates some medical professions and researchers. More often, it is about the one they could not. Someone very dear to them, who despite all effort, perished too soon.

In my work helping people to become better leaders, I sometimes encounter those who reject the term, leadership. Their belief system won't allow them to step up, face the burdens, nor accept the responsibility. It's disappointing, but reluctant leaders can be as equally harmful as lousy leaders, so, perhaps it is for the best.

No, the heart-wrenching tragedy occurs when someone with a powerful, servant leadership mentality, warm heart and giving spirit, repeatedly allows themselves to be taken advantage of by unappreciative leaders. While it is difficult to see those you care about flounder in any abusive or highly leveraged relationship; it's unbearable to see them slowly grow blind to the impact of their decisions. Incapable of breaking a destructive pattern, frenetic momentum builds until they suddenly become lousy leaders themselves.

When they cross that Rubicon, there is nothing more I can do. I sob over the loss, and for the knowledge that a new adversary is born. Despite the pain that accompanies this rare event, it reinforces my mission to disrupt, dismantle, and diminish the negative influence of lousy leaders.

Becoming a lousy leader is easy. Resist the temptation, lest we meet in unfavorable conditions.

## *Be Outspoken*

Diplomacy and tact are worthy pursuits. It doesn't harm you to slow down and provide a little thought before spouting off something that could be hurtful to others. There's no reason to be intentionally rude when making a point. When you've got the choice to be either kind or right, I agree, it's better to be kind. Nonetheless, I do not cheer shrinking violets. I prefer the candid and outspoken. There's a way to be kind AND blunt.

My mother was a worrywart, and though she may have kept her more vivid imaginations quiet to protect people from undue influence, she never shied away from sharing her opinion.

My stepmother's common sense and sound reasoning could cut like a stiletto, but you knew where you stood. She regularly shared her opinion and respected you enough to let you hang yourself with your own rope.

I worked with a guy who was a master of listening to his gut. If an interaction felt "off" or threatened to damage the relationship, he would stop, and with great candor, not let you go until everything was rebalanced.

I was married to a woman for over 24 years who struggled with the art of tact but handled difficult conversations with aplomb. Her approach was and remains refreshing.

Sometimes awkward, sometimes inappropriate, but always appreciated, these four people    and more, have solidified my preference for the outspoken. Even with incorrect assertions, the outspoken are masters at driving conversations toward the truth, spawning thought, and igniting action.

There are those who get offended — that taboos or unspeakable things are given voice, mores challenged, traditions upended.

Agreed, it can be jarring.

So what?

As long as the outspokenness comes from a good place, is not meant to cause harm, but illumination, bring it on.

Strengthen your resolve to give and receive feedback with grace and graciousness, and you will eliminate animosity, find quicker solutions to problems and destructive patterns, see with fresh eyes, and often build stronger more meaningful relationships.

Know your truth and be a voracious advocate for it. You have a preference, choose it. You have a voice, use it.

## *Rejecting Leadership*

There's a trend where a lot of good people are distancing themselves from the term, "leader," because it leaves a bad taste in their mouth.

What about you? Do you reject leadership?

I can't blame you, you might have lousy role models, be disillusioned with former heroes, or maybe it feels like too much of a burden.

The thing is, if you're a good leader, don't throw it away. The world needs you. I need you. See, I detest lousy leaders too, but the only way we can disrupt, dismantle, and diminish the influence they have, is by meeting them head-on with better leadership. You up for the challenge?

## *Two Lousy Leaders*

**When a good leader turns a blind eye to a bad leader, you have two lousy leaders.**

Life is full of difficult choices. Loyalty and honor are real but can get warped. Pay attention to who earns your loyalty and how you define honor. Does your code hurt more people then it protects? Have you allowed the thirst for money or status to become your master, and ignored your values? Do you betray your purpose by your actions or inactions?

Lists of injustices are easy to create. A good archbishop who protects a bad priest is far less holy than they believe. A good cop who defends a bad cop ceases to be a useful public servant.

Life is complicated and full of nuance. People have individual pressures and motivations we have no visibility into and have no claim to know better. However, common sense exists; right and wrong -- good and evil exist. You can argue for your perspective.

Do that.

Make your case for inaction, for protecting predators, enabling deceit, absolving arrogance. Lay out your reasons for tolerating the intolerable, accepting the unacceptable. Do not be silent and ignore the difficulties, or blithely consider it a nightmare from which you'll magically awake. Do not pray for the clock to run down so you can escape accountability.

Make whatever choices you need to feel whole. They are your choices. However, it would be foolish, should you take the easy, cowardly path, to consider yourself a leader.

## Don't Be Afraid to Lead

I come across a lot of capable people who are afraid to lead. Frequently they are blind to the fact that they are already leading. By having a vision, acting upon it, and gathering resources to help fulfill it, they are well on their way.

It starts with self-leadership. Some skip this step, but eventually, there is a reckoning and correction that requires attention here.

Then there is leading another individual. Successful partnerships of any kind are a dance between who leads, who follows, and when.

There are team and organizational leadership. Moreover, there is governance. You needn't ever take on these advanced roles to be considered a leader. You are a leader in your family, among friends, of a volunteer group or committee. Most importantly, especially if you have fear, you are responsible for leading yourself.

Study leadership. Get better at leading and following. Leadership is everywhere. When you get the chance to lead, I want you to take it, and I want you to lead well.

## *Empathy and Curiosity*

Empathy and curiosity are two traits a lousy leader can't comprehend. They are the same traits a great leader calls upon instinctively.

Empathy is about warmth first, even without fully understanding the predicament. It is grace and compassion when hearing of someone else's turmoil. It's not a rush to problem-solve. Judgments are deferred. It's pure heart and connection, if only for a moment. It costs the leader nothing and supplies those in pain a moment of ease.

Curiosity is the driving force of improvement. Ever increasing one's knowledge and then the knowledge of others, is a trait of a good leader. They seek to understand. It can be book smart, street smart, or a combination of the two. They investigate and seek answers to problems. They don't claim superior intellect, and they are always open to a better way. They are humble enough to not know something and confident enough to admit it, because they will always seek better solutions.

Be choosy with your leaders. One who lacks empathy and curiosity is not worthy of your following.

## *Must Be Present to Win*

Every day there's more history being made. It's important to learn from the past. How did others face challenges similar to your own?

The future is predictable only if we study patterns, test models, examine theories, and dare to imagine. The future remains unwritten with an abundance of chaos to wreak havoc on well-laid plans.

Your best course is to be mindful, aware, and present for every interaction and task. When you are present, you give empathy a chance to grow. The present is the only time and place you can exert personal control and mastery. Your attitude in the here and now is what most affects the there and then.

If you want to win, be present.

## *Passion on a Pedestal*

Stop seeking passion. It will elude you until it sees you working. What you are passionate about is the thing you are most willing to suffer for, enduring it for 10, 15, 20 years or more.

Passion is the endeavor you cannot stop doing. It consumes you. It doesn't have to energize you, that's a myth. It often drains you, but you seldom mind. It's not something that sparks at just the right moment. You're confusing passion for lust. There is a time and place for spontaneous ignition, but passion is an arduously slow smoldering burn. You cannot go out and find it because you already carry it with you. Its crucible rests inside you.

Vision is seeded in your fertile mind and birthed by your imagination. You envision a place or condition you want to change or create. You often fail in its pursuit, sometimes publicly. If the vision has no meaning for you, you abandon it, or worse, pursue it mindlessly. Passion is what gives your vision meaning and makes the suffering losses bearable. Those who have acknowledged their passion know the thought of being without it is more terrifying than any suffering it causes.

To nourish your vision, you count on your passion. To nourish your passion, you must take action. You must either act on, decide, or communicate the things that support your vision and passion or else you remain a dreamer, a starving artist ill-equipped to paint.

Action gives your imagination concrete feedback. Action makes you feel productive and satisfied. Passion does not feed you. Action does. Passion does not reward your efforts. Action does.

When you put passion on a pedestal, you rob vision and action of their equal due. If you insist on searching for passion, focus on taking consistent action. Passion will then predictably show itself, like a jealous muse desperate for attention. Acknowledge it, then get back to work.

## *New Day*

When you are on purpose, the dawn of each day is filled with potential and excitement. It's your chance to hit the reset button while countless others around you fumble for the snooze. Such is the power of a great goal. It fuels your mornings, no matter the season or day of the week.

The weak bemoan Mondays. Yes, they sacrifice their agency to a calendar and clock. They are the captains of rudderless ships. Their slack, bovine expressions do little to inspire confidence in their command.

Your work may not be glamorous. You may detest it, find it demeaning or difficult. But you do not allow yourself to be defined by your occupation. You bring definition to it with your attitude, attire, and approach. For these reasons, you excel and move ever closer to the life you imagine for yourself.

It begins with you and how you greet each day. Good morning.

## *Don't Just Sit There. Think about it.*

When was the last time you thought?
I'm not talking about dwelling, regretting, wishing, or worrying. I'm talking about honest to goodness, calorie burning, serious thinking. Not scenario planning and what-iffing, not endless rumination. Critical, logical thinking.

Not meditation and mindfulness. Yes, it's good to practice both and live in the moment. But you're not doing that right now either.

Try some active sitting. You've got the whole, "let the world wash over you" down pat. Now, steer the ship. Pick the direction you want to go and THINK about how you're going to get there.

Will you travel alone or with others? Is this a secret or do you need to broadcast your plans for greater support? Do you have the right provisions and skills, or do you need to learn or hire along the way? Is your attitude in check, your appearance appropriate to the task, and your approach aligned with your purpose? Are you acting on purpose, or by habit?

There's something important to you. You know what it is because it just fluttered across your mind. Capture it and give it some thought.
Thought is the nourishment your ideas need to grow. Start feeding them.

## *Be a Better Gatekeeper*

Stop taking random advice from people.

Be a better gatekeeper and pay attention to those who make you think, laugh, and take action. Preferably all three.

We have such excellent access to knowledge, new perspectives, and views of the world. It's easy to take it for granted and let it all stream past us. There's no shortage of people spouting off their insights and opinions, present company included. Each pontificator has their reasons, from noble to nefarious. Your job, a new responsibility for many, is to act as a gatekeeper.

Keep the toxicity away, unless you are studying it. Have a broad circle that confirms your thinking, to give you support when you need it, but also include those who challenge you. You should have your beliefs challenged, if for no other reason than to strengthen them. Find ideas from a world beyond your own, and you will see similar goals and differing paths. Your competitors will raise your game, and your detractors will keep you humble.

Do not rely on others to edit your inputs. Find the sources you know, like, and trust and compare them to those you don't. The truth you seek and need to hear will nearly always rest between those two camps.

Do not be a passive observer. Participate. First, have the courage to speak. Then, endeavor to be heard.

## *Your 90 Day Review*

1. Review the last 90 days of your life. You set some big goals — how ya doing? Do you need to adjust them? Don't go smaller. Reach higher.

2. You met new people. Did anyone positively influence your life, your goals, your success? Have you appreciate them?

3. Where have you spent your time and money? These give a hint as to what you value. Knowing that, will anything change?

4. What have you tolerated that you swore you would stop putting up with? What fear have you conquered, challenge overcome, talent strengthened?

5. What commitments have you made but not yet kept? What promises have you delivered?

6. What have you learned about yourself?

7. What actions, decisions, and communications do you need to complete to feel good about yourself?

8. How have you celebrated your successes and near successes?

9. What do you want to do, have, or be in the next 90 days? Don't shrug; you know the answer. Leaders don't shrug. Leaders lead. Make your plan and then go for wins every day. You've got 90 opportunities.

## *Harmony Over Balance*

I don't like the personal development industry's "Wheel of Life" because I think balance is the wrong thing to attempt to achieve. Have you ever tried to accomplish perfect balance? Balancing anything is difficult and all-consuming. The practice requires precision, patience, and a bottomless supply of trial and error. These traits aren't inherently bad, but you don't want to use them on something a grand as your life. The attempts are distracting, typically fruitless, and let's be honest, sucks the joy out of the moment. What's the alternative?

Harmony.

Use whatever criteria you consider to be the critical elements of your life (I've included suggestions below) and rate your current satisfaction in each.

There's not a right or wrong. You don't need 10s across the board. Think of them collectively like an equalizer on a stereo and decide what works for you. If you like heavy bass, adjust to your taste and the needs of the moment, (which could be a month, a season, a decade.)

Harmony is more pleasant than balance and infinitely easier to achieve. A new phase in life? New priorities? Recalibrate the equalizer.

1. Explore your self-perceptions

Examples of someone highly satisfied might look like this:

- Financial - Financially independent and free from financial stress. Satisfied with your current level of income.

- Career - A fulfilling and nourishing career. On a positive career path.

- Health - In great shape. Receiving effective healthcare. Exercising regularly and eating for sustenance and pleasure, not emotional comfort.

- Relationships - Pleased and content with current relationships. Loved by the people who mean the most to you.

- Contribution - Giving of yourself to others.

- Recreation - Spend leisure time enjoying your interests. Relaxation, refreshment, and pleasure.

- Education - Engaged in creative and stimulating mental activities. Use resources available to expand knowledge.

- Personal - Evolving, not just improving, because you continually experiment.

2. Rate your current level of satisfaction in each dimension of your life with a score between 0 (Very Dissatisfied) and 10 (Highly Satisfied) and Plot your current level of satisfaction.

3. Record your three highest and lowest rated areas.

4. Why are these your highest and lowest rated areas?

5. Did you notice any trends or themes?

6. Given these scores, what two areas are you willing to improve over the next six months to make the most significant difference in your life?

Congratulations, answering these questions will give you more insight and self- reflection than most people will invest in a year. Now, act on purpose.

## *13 Months*

I keep a baker's dozen of empty Wellbutrin bottles in my closet and look at them once in awhile, to remind myself of the 13 months of hellish depression I went through several years ago.

The cause doesn't matter. Once depression grabs you by the throat, or seemingly the soul, you don't care about the reasons. When you are in the depths, burning the last package of Pop-Tarts in the toaster, or running out of Nutella could set you back. It is unpredictable and unimaginable. After a couple of doses of medication, my equilibrium faltered, and unfathomably, I felt worse. I knew I'd have to give my body time to regulate and adjust. On days I could summon the energy I exercised, meditated, listened to music, and all the other things people recommend. I was not adverse to anything, because I was too apathetic to raise an objection. Nothing held pleasure nor excitement.

My kids saved me with their laughter, stories, and curiosity about the world; and the fact that I needed to hold it together for them. I created important habits, like dinners with plenty of discussion about the day, goals, and future planning. I posted our family charter, which they helped craft. I welcomed meals from family and friends, and long phone calls with those who checked in. Every day was sluggish, sad, and punctuated with tears which leaked from my eyes without notice or cause.

There was also laughter. I worked, I wrote, I created nearly every day, even with the burdensome weight on my chest. I felt fraudulent. How could I advise others to manage better and lead well if I couldn't manage my own affairs? With help and time, I learned I *was* managing. Each day I did not succumb to dark thoughts was a victory, and those victories began to stack up. Inevitably, something in life would knock them over and throw me back. I could retreat to the corner, curl up into a weeping ball, or I could stand and persist, still weeping. I permitted myself to be vulnerable, to allow each emotion to wash over me. I was committed to learning from the experience, not ignore or deny its existence.

Thirteen months is a blink of the eye that takes place over an eternity. The daily battles were real, unwanted, and not simply thought away with happy platitudes. Depression is hellish, and it is conquerable, although your pride will not serve you. You need others.

I can be fairly stubborn, and I was not going to allow myself to be defeated. Even when the bleak fogginess enveloped my head and robbed my passion, I trudged through to meet my demons, looked them in the eye, flashed an FU signal, and hissed, *"Not today. You don't get me today."*

So many ailments, diseases, and epidemics plague our fellow citizens. Find one to help defeat. Do not sit on the sidelines while others are plunged into private hells. Begin to lead. Be a persistent, dogged opponent of the things that cause pain and suffering. Help others to know, it gets better.

## *Visceral Leadership*

I have a visceral reaction to leadership that has never let me down. It operates on both extremes of the continuum.

It's no secret that lousy leadership pisses me off; not only because these type of leaders tend to be arrogant dicks, but because they don't take their responsibility seriously. They have a direct adverse effect on people; and their negligence screws up the careers and aspirations of those who fall under their influence. Either through ignorance or intent, they can be counted on to take advantage of others; feed self-doubt, exploit talent and resources, belittle contributions, withhold basic appreciation, and scoff at common manners and professionalism. They get away with it, why? Because they are good in a specialized field? They can make money or structure deals? The industry-specific skills they possess are baseline requirements, not enormous differentiators for which they should be lauded.

Lousy leaders are easily and quickly identifiable for me. So too, are effective leaders. These people are the opposite, putting others before self, solving problems whether they are affected or not. They praise progress, express love, encourage ideas, share dreams and treat people with dignity. They instinctively express random acts of leadership. It is their lifestyle -- their calling, and leaves me in awe; stirred with positive emotion. I hold back tears of joy and shake with excitement, not frustration or anger.

There are many good leaders in all walks of life. Lousy leaders know this and try to keep them in their place with predictable and sad tactics. 1 work with those who can become great leaders before the lousy leaders grind away their gifts. I don't always get there in time, and it saddens me deeply. However I too, do my best, don't give up, and intend to prevail. There will always be lousy leaders, but great leaders can reduce their destructive influence every day.

## *How Do You Invest Your Time Over a Long Weekend?*

**Remembering**? This weekend, you will no doubt make time to remember fallen heroes.

**Reconnecting**? Do you make time to reach out to family, friends and the other important people in your life?

**Relaxing**? Will you spend time in a hammock or a garden just chilling, or being productive?

**Recovering**? Have you been a slacker on your goals or commitments? Long weekends are a great time to play catch up.

**Reading**? There is a time and place for recreational reading, but what about studying a subject you would like to learn more about.

**Advancing**? Will you use the time that your competitors and naysayers are sleeping, drinking, vacationing away, as an opportunity to pass them?

*Time is a gift. Appreciate it daily.*

## "Let Me Fail"

I recently shared dinner with a dear friend who was about to embark on a new adventure. She alternated between bouts of excitement and nervousness, possessing the natural joy that comes from stretching outside your comfort zone, coupled with the sudden pang of uncertainty.

Naysayers and provocateurs cling to that uncertainty and over inflate dread to make you second guess yourself and bring your lofty goals down to their level. Those with wanderlust and unconditional love, discount the nerves and excitedly celebrate with you and share effortless support.

Despite my aspirations, I am not perfect and cowardly played both roles. Admittedly, I was acting overprotective; a trait usually grounded in good intentions, but seldom expressed well. I had convinced myself to be devil's advocate to stir the pot, challenge assumptions, and validate her convictions -- none of which were any of my business, nor did I have any right to do. To the other extreme, I did share in her enthusiasm and marveled over the bravery, talent, intelligence and grit she had to pursue her dreams and enhance her knowledge. I would be a hypocrite if I were not supportive. How could I do anything but applaud? We playfully argued points and counterpoints. I had complete faith in her ability to be successful in any endeavor, AND I had sadness around her desire to leave what is for what could be.

My heart soared and all disagreements vanished when she finally said, "Let me fail."
It was not a request for permission, nor a premonition. It was simply, a firm statement and a beautiful expression that summed up what I believe to be powerful leadership.

You must always allow people to develop and expand their capacity, pursue their interests, and support their dreams. If you do not, they will leave you and never return. If you do, they may still leave you, but they will find ways to express gratitude and share their newfound knowledge with you in ways you never imagined.

Letting people fail is about autonomy, trust, and faith. During those times when your paths share in the journey, be a strong leader. Be confident, secure, and respect the needs of others to forge their own way. Allow people the space to do extraordinary things on their terms, while still supporting the bigger vision. Never stand in the way of someone's personal development.

When someone demonstrates leadership by his or her willingness to take risks and face failure with their eyes wide open; honor them. They are taking ownership of their decisions and actions. If you fight them, you lose. If you show love and support, you both win, regardless of any success or failure.

Besides, anyone who says, "let me fail," most assuredly will not fail in anything that matters, because they already have a winning attitude and are willing to take action.

Be the kind of leader who fosters that environment and you and those you encounter will thrive.

## *How You Become Successful Matters*

People who want to take the easy way out tend to get mad at me, and those who feel rudderless get frustrated with me when I remind them that success requires achieving the desired results AND helping others along the way.

I make no room for rainmakers whose behavior routinely cause their coworkers to cry. It's not enough to deliver results. It's not enough to treat people with respect, dignity, and give them room to grow - perhaps beyond you. To be an effective leader you do all of that, and more.

Becoming successful, however you define it for yourself, is great, but do not get lulled into thinking there is only one path.

Avoid putting people whose success you admire, on a pedestal. Lousy leaders can be very successful, but there is a toll and someone, usually someone innocent, must pay.

Results are important -- how you achieve them are more important.

Become discerning. Stop considering people who lie or swindle, to be great negotiators. The fact that they had to lie and swindle proves that they are not. Because someone has acquired riches is not sufficient cause to emulate them if their achievement occurs by dishonorable means. Devoting valuable time to learn their darker skills may cause you more harm than it is worth.

We are imperfect beings prone to shade the truth, lookout for self interests, and make questionable decisions from time to time. We are human, and mistakes in judgment happen. I'm talking about the habitual behaviors some engage in to create their "success" whether it be amassing fame, fortune, or power. You can achieve these things without being a dick.

Great leaders care about people AND results. Lousy leaders care only about one of those.

Good faith negotiators know the tricks lousy deal makers try to pull, and easily thwart them. Those who are wealthy in their heart first, make a greater positive impact on the people around them. Those who rely heavily on their wealth to define their worth, will ceaselessly chase more often at the detriment to or on the backs of, others. Lousy leaders are consumed with self-serving power plays, while better leaders are compelled to help others become more powerful.

Reinforce your moral code, particularly when times are hard, choices difficult, or the temptation for the "easy way" too great. Resist the urge to feed the ego of lousy leaders by cooing over their so-called success. Yes, these douche bags can be charismatic and exciting, but they don't need to be enriched by your devotion. Instead, starve them with a lack of attention and invest in those with stronger character and kind hearts. Invest in yourself. Your success matters.

## *You've Got This*

Great leaders do not get that way overnight. They face obstacles and the temptation to take the easy way out. Unlike lousy leaders, they do not succumb when things get difficult.

Effective leaders persevere through crisis and stay fixated on their goal, not the path. As your challenges grow, so do you. It would be nice if you sustained your confidence, but it will waver from time to time. You will feel like a poser, inadequate to the task, and question your ability. The answer will always be, "You've got this."

You have strengths far greater than you use. You put your faith many places; it is time to put it in yourself. When you find your goal, vision, purpose, or values tested today, don't hide. Stand up for them. You've got this.

## *Alone, or with Your Flock, Soar*

Sometimes you have to be independent and chart your own course. You will fly high, and far, and have a broad perspective on your world, up above the fray.

Other times, you will want company, share resources, communicate with your friends, cheer each other on, and stay nearer to the ground, so you do not miss any opportunities.

The choice is yours. You will rely on either your head or your heart, instinct or common sense. Ultimately, your decision may be right, or it may be wrong, but only you can make it. Own it and soar.

## *Why? Because!*

Once you become an adult, there's something you can stop doing, but most don't. It is important to know your *why* - the motivation, inspiration, reason that compels you to pursue the big goal in your life. It helps you to understand why, but you do not have to justify it to anyone else.

Others will ask, press, and many will get frustrated if you do not answer them. They can. Let them. Your why is personal to you. Everyone else will judge it and directly or indirectly, try to talk you out of it.

Most people will chip away at your why, question your motive, or flat out tell you that you are wrong. Even the well-intentioned will tread here. It is human nature. Under that pressure you forget, it is YOUR why, not theirs. Some of your critics might be right. It does not matter. You are the one who lives with your why, and as an adult takes responsibility for it and owns the consequences, both positive and negative.

If you are pursuing your wants and desires, that is sufficient reason. You may fail, you could be misguided, perhaps a touch delusional; or you could be a brilliant pioneer. Neither matters.

All that matters is that you pursue your why because you have decided you WANT to.

Congratulations, you are starting to act like a leader.

## *Enjoy Leading or Don't Lead*

Not every day is sunshine and unicorns. Leading is not always fun. You need to make tough decisions between choices that aren't any good. That is what leaders do. If you thought it was giving commands to people to satisfy your whim, you goofed.

You are going to have good days, horrible days, and days that make you go, "meh." Enjoy them all. It is better than the alternative.

When leading feels like a burden or drudgery to you, it is time to hand over the reins. There are enough joyless leaders. We need more happy warriors filled with gratitude for what is, optimism for what can be, and the energy and innovation to bring it about.

Need more confidence and support to manage better and lead well? Reach out to Consulting; we know where to find it in you.

## *No Refuge for Poor Leaders*

If you pay someone for advice and they caution you against hiring a capable and attractive person of the opposite sex so that you may protect yourself and resist temptation, fire them.

If you take their advice or have hesitated to hire qualified people you thought were attractive because it would be too big of a risk, resign from any leadership role immediately. You have failed at basic professionalism, self-control, and discipline.

You likely lack empathy, situational awareness, and have a wavering moral character. I will go on a limb and guess you are probably also a jackass to work with, but maybe no one has told you yet.

Reassess your behaviors, values, and beliefs if you want to avoid career derailment. Fail to correct your ways, and you may find cover amongst other lousy leaders, but you will not prevail. Effective leaders do not provide refuge to poor leaders for long. It's time to manage better and lead well.

## *Walk with Purpose, Not Confusion*

You will not know where you are headed every moment of every day. Life is full of surprises that will push you off track, distract you, or lead you in an entirely new direction.

Know your purpose and be undeterred. Relish the adventure of the unknown for it will teach you.

On those lazy days filled with more strolls than strides, keep your purpose in mind, and you will still make progress.

## *Leadership Ingredients*

There are lots of attributes they say a leader should have. Ignore them.

Those attributes are the seasoning that gives the meal a pleasant flavor. As a leader, concern yourself with the proper nutrition first, then spice it up. Otherwise, it is empty calories and wasted effort.

To be effective, know your personal purpose and values and live them. Then, have a vision, passion, and action surrounding what you're leading.

Miss any of these ingredients and you have mush.

## *You Always Make a Difference*

If you don't think you do ... keep thinking until you find a way you can. Then go do that.

You won't always know how, when, or why, but you will always make a difference.

You won't always know who, or what is affected by your actions, but it is impossible for you to avoid mattering.

Everything you do matters to someone else somewhere. Do not settle for always being a passenger during this journey. Be of service to others, find a wrong to right, a wound to heal, tears to turn into laughter.

You are gifted with the ability to make a difference, make them positive.

What I want you to do is, work on your purpose, live your values, and lead well.

When you work on *your* purpose, you automatically become more productive, happier, and act with gratitude.

When you live *your* values, you make better decisions based off your beliefs, goals, and wants.

When you lead well, you are remaining curious, optimistic, empathetic, and persistent. You are faithful to *your* mission, and freely share insights for the betterment of others.

When you apply clear vision, passion, and action to each endeavor, you contribute a greater piece of *yourself* to the world.

All of this grows your confidence, personal power, and capacity to lead – yourself and others.

Lousy leaders cannot accomplish these feats. Which is why *you* must.

## *Lead the Change or Lead the Same*

Want to change things?
Lead the change.

Don't want things to change?
Lead the same.

You can sit back and be a nonparticipating observer 95% of the time. You will either remain blissful or stew in resentment; depending upon your attitude and point of view. You can have gratitude for the luxury of living in contentment, or complacency. Occasionally you will get riled up enough that you will feel compelled to lead.

I prefer working with those who roll up their sleeves and get involved 95% of the time, and are content 5% of the time. It is when they rejuvenate that they most often get struck by another cause, vision, or idea to bring about or contribute.

I'm not overly picky about when you choose to lead, but I care passionately that when you do, you manage better and lead well.

## *Sometimes You Are Wrong*

You are not infallible. You make mistakes. It is an uncomfortable feeling, knowing you goofed. Many people try to avoid the sensation of being wrong by never speaking up, never standing up, never venturing into the unknown. They feel safe and secure at first, but as these actions -- or lack of actions -- become a habit, that security is replaced with regret. What was once simply uncomfortable now induces fear.

What if you get rejected? You will be humiliated if you are wrong. You have to be perfect.

Most rejection is not personal, but sometimes it is. It stings, but you can recover if you give yourself permission to heal.

When you have strong integrity, attacks to your self-respect and dignity are fruitless because you do not allow breaches.

You cannot be perfect. It is an illusion. You can be in a realm that is acceptable. There is a zone of "mostly right" that you can aim for. Do that.

Being wrong can hurt your pride -- when it does, know that you are focused in the wrong direction. When you are wrong, you probably hurt someone else. Either you did not listen to them attentively, or you disregarded their emotions or beliefs. Apologize. Make amends if you can. Repair the damage. You will not always be forgiven for your error, but you will recover. You must if you want to get better at what you do.

**Being wrong is inevitable. Stop fearing mistakes by managing better and leading well.**

## *Be The Better Option*

You defeat lousy leadership with better leadership.
Be the better option.

Smug rhetoric and incoherent arguments do not contain better ideas. Fear and paranoia driven tirades do not beckon better angels. Sowing chaos as a management technique is as childish as throwing tantrums and promoting angry fervor instead of confronting facts and resolving challenges.

Whining, complaining without providing an alternative, retreating into the shadows, are not better options and only serve to strengthen the grip of lousy leaders.

It can be tiresome, so some retire; they no longer possess the energy to battle the lousy leaders, who sprout like bramble across the paths of progress. That is why you need to become a better leader.

Summon the help of those experienced but weary; you will need their wisdom to spare you from costly missteps. You do not have to fear making mistakes of your own, by being equipped with unwavering purpose, core values, and enough humility to apologize and make amends if required.

Stay curious and attentive. Retain your integrity by confronting lousy leadership, whether borne by ignorance or intent. Provide better ideas. Be the better option.

## *Be Ready to Lead*

Ever sit with a bunch of people and awkwardly talk about what to do next? Everyone is tentative and polite. No one wants to offend or look foolish. People are going out of their way to avoid disagreements and confrontation.

And that is only trying to decide what to have for lunch!

Everyone has a good intent -- keeping others happy to sustain the status quo. The problem is, the status quo is unsustainable. Eventually, lunchtime is over, and no one ate. Now performance for the rest of the day is shot, and some people are resentful of others and beating themselves up for not making a decision.

Next day, same room. One person is polite but not tentative. They do not think about acting foolish or offending people, not because they are careless, but because their concern for such things matches the level of the decision being made. They may not enjoy disagreements and confrontation, but they do not shy away from them. They know navigating differences is how to achieve preferences. This person declares a lunch spot and then acts. Some, likely most, will follow. Some will not, for a myriad of legitimate reasons. That does not prevent anyone from eating.

Leaders lead, no matter the circumstance. Given the opportunity, they take it. They adjust to the results. In cases bigger or smaller than lunch, don't sit around. Be ready to lead.

## *Something Missing?*

You know those times when you feel like things just aren't right? Things aren't firing on all cylinders. You're not panicking, but your frustration is growing. You feel stumped because you cannot figure it out. Things should be going better, but something is missing.

Check your leadership.

If something is awry, the thing that is most likely missing is your leadership. Perhaps you're not providing any, or maybe there is a mismatch between the kind of leadership you possess and the kind that the situation requires.

You might be over thinking and under acting. Perhaps you are impetuous when patience is required. You can't be expected to see your blind spots; as the name implies, you have limited vision. You have to broaden your perspective.

Take responsibility, take ownership, and take your leadership seriously. Start to use it more effectively, and you'll find solutions to your problems.

## *Monday Excitement*

If you aren't excited each Monday, you're working on the wrong stuff. Act on purpose.

You don't HAVE to like your job. Few people get excited about their commute and interacting with busybody coworkers, always asking about their weekend plans. Most people, as many as 80% according to some surveys, have a lousy boss who they dread being around. It's rare to have company pride and feel like you're being looked after and cared about when your friends get mistreated or laid off. When people are asked how they are doing, and the most common responses are, "Back to the grind," "We're halfway there," and, "At least it's Friday," we've got a problem.

It's okay to love the weekend, not because it's not work, but because it gives you a chance to pursue your passions. In many cases, the job you hate funds the lifestyle you want. That's not ideal, the trade is not balanced, but few people negotiate well, so it's what they accept.

Stop tolerating mediocrity in your life. Ideally, you're getting paid and building a career off of something you like. If you're not, you ought to think about making better goals instead of excuses, regardless of your age. When you're sacrificing your purpose (and often your values) for people and a cause you don't believe it or are even ambivalent about, you are not going to perform well. This subpar performance seeps into every area of your life. The reverse is also true. If you are acting on purpose, supporting your values for a cause and people you believe in, you are productive and happy. This optimal state of being seeps into every area of your life.

You have a choice, every moment of every day … but let's start with Monday. You can begin to alter your outlook and find ways to bring your passion, productivity, and purpose with you. It's a new week. Go make great things happen. Don't act out of habit, desperation, or fear. Act with purpose.

## *Luck and Good Fortune*

Instead of looking for luck and good fortune for yourself, why don't you secretly provide it to others?

Typically you have to work to grow your fortune. Some people have to work harder, and they earn less, while others seem to stumble into success. Many dream of lottery winnings and how it could change their lives. The chance of success disproportionate to effort made is low but does exist, so people continue to wish and hope and pray.

A better strategy; help others – as many as you can, as often as you can. Don't exclude yourself – you'll have no effectiveness if you don't take care of yourself.

Increase your efforts, help others and your luck and fortune will grow

## *Are You Acting On Purpose?*

I believe happiness and purposefulness come about by the active pursuit of a worthy goal. Therefore if you want to be happy, you should never be without a great goal.

Imagine if every woman, man, and child you know had at least one great goal that they were actively working toward every day? The buzz of energy produced from such productivity, collaboration, and purposefulness would likely do more than illuminate cities; it would illuminate minds long shrouded in a fog of doubt. It would raise hope, lift spirits, and propel those with a success mindset ever forward. To solve what others thought unsolvable. To achieve what all but a few thought unattainable. To refuse the deferment of dreams long-held, or thoughts long held silent. To try, to fail, to try again, without stigma or scorn.

It is possible.

We may not ever live in a world without conflict, but we cannot call it living if it's in a world without goals. The best we could do then is exist, and merely existing is not good enough for me, and I doubt it is for you.

What's your next great goal? Will you pursue it with joy?
Take our Purpose Self-Assessment to see if you're on track.

## *How You Doin'?*

When was the last time you asked someone how they were doing?

Here's how you can tell if someone is more concerned with power than they are with good leadership.

Someone concerned with power is going to use "I" and "Me" when they speak. When they talk to you, they will tell you what they are doing, feeling, thinking and may pause to ask you how you think they are doing, thinking, or feeling. That's lousy leadership.

Someone who is an effective leader is going to use the words "You" and "We" when they speak. They use "I" a lot too, mostly to claim responsibility. They nearly always keep the conversation off of their accomplishments and on your goals and dreams. Hence, "How are you doing?" isn't a nicety, it's genuine curiosity and caring. They prefer to talk about you and search for ways to aid you in your pursuits.

So the next time you start a conversation, pay attention to who you're caring most about.

## *Never Feel Lost*

When you know your **purpose** and **values**, you feel great about making decisions that support who you want to be and where you want to go.

When you set your mind on your **dreams** and you **celebrate** along the way, you are making progress.

If you ever feel lost, any one of these set points can guide you. Know them all, and you'll have complete confidence in your voyage.

## *Fix It*

Good leaders know when they've goofed up. Not right away — but eventually, they know. They ask for feedback, pay attention to criticism, and are astute to the things NOT being said.

So what happens when you realize you've goofed; when your judgment, behavior, or assumption, was wrong?

A lousy leader does nothing because they are incapable of seeing reality. If they make mistakes, they don't apologize, because they think apologies are a sign of weakness. That's why they ultimately fail. They care more about themselves than those they have hurt.

If you've been a crappy leader lately, or even have a suspicion that you might be slipping in your purpose, values, or goals, what should you do?

Fit it.

Figure it out and fix it.

Ask for help and fix it.

Make fixing it a priority.

Your integrity is at risk, and more than that, you're causing pain to other people.

Fix it.

## *Great Goal*

Want to build your strength, confidence, and integrity? Set a great goal for yourself and achieve it.

You don't have to tell anyone else,
but you do have to write it down.

You don't have to include others in your plan,
but you've got to have a plan.

You don't have to talk about it,
but you do have to look at your goal and plan every single day.

You don't have to post updates publicly,
but you have to make progress, big or small, every single day.

You don't have to suffer in silence,
you can reward yourself for little wins along the way.

When you don't work on your own goals, you work on someone else's. There's nothing wrong with that; the best leaders serve others.

However … you need a great goal of your own to keep you focused on your purpose, strengthen your skills, grow your confidence, and build your integrity.

Never be without a great goal.

## *You Don't Need Permission to Lead*

You don't need permission to lead.
You need a purpose.

Don't wait to be anointed or appointed. Lead from where you are.
If the purpose is important to you, if the timing and circumstances are right, you must rise.

Prepare, knowing you will never be fully prepared. You will be attacked by those who were too fearful to stand themselves. Expect it, even welcome it, for their challenges will strengthen your resolve and character. Seeing this, others will join you. Accept their help and support with grace and gratitude.

Step out from behind the curtain of doubt and take your place on the stage. Speak up and be heard. Not for the applause, which can intoxicate you; for the cause, which will improve the status quo.

Do not lead for money or fame, grandeur or power.
Lead for those who need you in the darker hours.

Lead for those who've not found their voice, the multitudes who've lost their choice.

Lead in ways to grow and create, not restrict and deny.

Lead, to make things better in ways large and small.

Lead, to bring impossible dreams to within reach.

Lead, because you are compelled to lead and act on purpose.

These do not require permission. They only require you.

## *Head and Heart in Leadership*

If you can't choose between the head and the heart, pick the heart and trust the head to find a way to figure it out.

Maybe this seems off topic for a leadership advisor. It's not. If you're leading without heart, you're doing it wrong.

The heart is where you find love, soul, and inspiration. The heart is home to respect, esteem, empathy, humanity. It's where we find our purpose and our passion.

The head is where we entertain logic, judgment, safety, and preservation. The head is risk-averse. It prefers you to progress at a moderate pace, obey the rules and customs, and avoid rocking the boat.

Motivation is created in your head.
Inspiration is created in your heart.
Your head also creates fear and doubt.
Your heart is fearless and certain.

A good leader will make time to strategize options. The head thrives here because it likes to solve problems – and usually does.

A great leader also listens to their heart – although most will credit their gut. They have an inner knowing, and although it may not appear logical or sensible to others, they pursue this "feeling" if only because it "feels right."

Trust this feeling more often. Be open to input, feedback, and advice from others who may be more objective, so you have a complete picture, then proceed anyway. Lead with your heart and then let the head do its job.

## Are You Bad for Business?

Treating your employees poorly is not only lousy leadership, it's bad for business.

1. If you're a manager, supervisor, leader — anyone who has a team, and you treat them poorly, that's one strike. You're messing up your role.

2. If you can't recognize that a poorly treated team is going to reduce productivity and negatively impact the business, that's two strikes. You're messing up your fiduciary responsibility to the success of the organization.

3. If you're confused by parts 1 and 2 and think others are there to serve you, that's strike three. You have a poor concept of leadership and should return to an individual contributor role immediately before you cause more damage.

It's not too late. You can manage better and lead well … if you want to.

If you don't, someone else will.

## *Don't Wait to be Empowered*

Empowerment is great, and I don't mean to split hairs, but I've never liked the word. It implies power is being given to you by someone else. Yes, I suppose you can bestow that gift to yourself, give yourself permission to rise up, take authority, make decisions, etc. but it's still rooted in someone else (with power) loaning you some of theirs.

The problem is, those who make loans eventually want to be repaid, usually with interest. (And your best interest is not usually what they are looking after.) That's where it gets messy.

Skip all that.

Don't wait to be empowered. You have agency. Own it.

Be powerful now.

## *Raise Your Standards*

Anyone who devalues you, your ambitions your contributions, or your talents, has no place in your life. Raise your standards and minimize their influence on you.

Lousy leaders do this all the time. They treat you like they're doing you a favor. They belittle your ambitions, barely recognize your contributions, and ignore your talents. Sometimes friends and loved ones do this too. Don't tolerate it in them. They are protecting their interests, not promoting yours.

They have too much leverage over you; financial, psychological, emotional, physical, and they use it to extract compliance from you.

Sometimes you're stuck.

Endure what you must, but make it a goal to regain your personal power. They are abusing theirs, stop letting them rob you of yours. Detach from them and trade up to those who celebrate, challenge, educate, and honor you and your unique abilities.

Never stop doing this.

## *It Starts with Purpose*

Want to be a good business owner, executive, or friend? Know your purpose.

Want to be a good lover, companion, or spouse? Know your purpose.

Want to be a good investor of time, talent or treasure? Know your purpose.
Want to manage well and lead better? Know your purpose.

Everything starts with purpose. If you don't know yours, you'll flounder under someone else's. To learn your purpose, you need to be vulnerable, courageous, and honest. Until you do that, you will not lead well.

Begin to act on purpose, not by mistake.

Lots of people don't know their purpose, so they follow other people's purpose.
Eventually, they feel hollow and unfulfilled.

Lots of people don't know their core values, so they take on other people's values.
Eventually, they feel distraught and unsettled.
Lousy leaders take advantage or those who feel hollow, unfulfilled, distraught, and unsettled.

Effective leaders work diligently to replace those feelings with depth, fulfillment, focus, excitement, and clarity.
Work on your purpose and know your values every day. Let them guide you, inform your decisions, and inspire your life. They are yours alone. You don't have to explain them. Live them and be a great version of YOU.

## *Five Reasons Why Some Executives Do Not Put Poor Performing Leaders on Corrective Action*

Most people do not enjoy paperwork, and they like confrontation even less. Effective leaders are no different, but they take a deep breath and do it regardless. Lousy leaders do not. Here are five reasons some of these lousy leaders don't put poor performers on corrective action.

### Arrogance
An arrogant leader holds the belief that if one of their managers needs help with a problem they should be smart enough to fix it themselves. The arrogant leader seems to think that if they merely utter a command, and wave their hand, underlings will *"just handle it."* This seldom works well. If people knew how to fix their performance shortcomings, they would. When they do not have the confidence, ability or knowledge, they cannot make the required changes. Makes sense, right? If you are leading someone, a big part of improving their performance rests with you.

### Fearfulness
When a poor performer excels in one area of their job that directly benefits their immediate manager, they often get a lot of cover. Think of the rainmaking sales person who always manages to close the big deals. Sure, they make support staff cry with their rudeness or are late and disruptive to important meetings, but because they bring economic value, they often get a pass on their crappy behavior. Poor managers will easily justify the conduct by saying it is not so bad in the grand scheme of things, or by imagining how it could be much worse. Fear based thinking is cowardly and selfish. The lousy leader does not want to risk harming the goose that lays the golden eggs. By contrast, effective leaders do not tolerate any poor behavior which runs counter to the organization's values, norms, and culture. They will not hesitate to sacrifice short-term gains for the longer-term success of the team.

### Cluelessness
Lousy leaders regularly get caught by surprise. *"No one could have ever suspected this would happen?"* is a familiar refrain. It is a big hint that their inner circle of influence contains sycophants or weak leaders with poor persuasion skills. Between the worrywarts who think of everything that could go wrong, to the strategic-minded who continuously look for obstacles,

someone always suspects the worse case scenario. The leader may have lacked nuance and the ability to see the challenge with their own eyes, or they may have ignored the warnings that others provided. Because they have not been paying attention, they cannot see the problem so they will not admit to the problem. Effective leaders are proactive and attempt to correct behaviors or systems failures before they become problems.

## Negligence

A lousy leader will allow the poor behavior to continue because they do not want to be bothered with the work required to lead properly. They subscribe to the belief that *"things have a way of working themselves out."* These types of leaders and managers do not address, or document infractions and they probably do an equally poor job with recognition and reward. It is negligence to the basic tenets of effective leadership and relationship management.

## Abdication

Leaders are human beings, and it is unrealistic to expect perfection. There will always be some element of procrastination or avoidance of unpleasant tasks. However, when it becomes pervasive and habitual, it converts to an abdication of the role. Lousy leaders are often hesitant or refuse to admit, that as the leader, they too are in part responsible for the performance of their team members. They regularly shift blame to others because they do not want to put in the necessary work to improve the situation. An effective leader understands responsibility. They begin with the premise that a problem is fundamentally their fault and then they quickly explore ways to find a remedy.

There are many executives with strong character and integrity who take their role seriously and work with their leaders, formally and informally, to improve performance. They are the unacknowledged heroes who work to defeat lousy, predatory, and sometimes unlawful leadership in their midst in real time. An act that comes with risk and often without public reward. Endeavor to be that kind of leader.

## *Knowing Your Values*

Here's why knowing your values is so important. When you know them, you make decisions faster, and those decisions support you, they don't sabotage you. You know the difference between when you are acting congruent with your values, and when you are straying because your body tells you.

When things aren't right, you don't feel right. Curiosity becomes anxiety. Self-assuredness is replaced with doubt. Butterflies in your stomach no longer flutter, they punch. If you ignore the signs, they don't fully go away; you just grow used to them.

This is not where you find confidence, nor good leadership. When you know your values, you know what you want.

When you are a leader, you tell people what you want.

When the answer is yes, you show gratitude and keep moving forward.

When the answer is no, it can sting, but it is better to know no now, not later. You still show gratitude and move in a different direction.

Your values make it possible, so make time to get to know them better.

## *You Can Thank Your Lousy Boss*

You have worked for a lousy boss at some point in your career. You've had a manager, supervisor, professor, or teacher who not only didn't "get" you; they did not seem to interact well with anyone else either.

Maybe you felt like they micromanaged you, or maybe they were never around when you needed them. Perhaps they were so stringent with rules and procedures, you and your team never got a chance to use your talents to problem solve or innovate. Maybe they were recalcitrant and seemed to break every rule and norm imaginable, perhaps even engaging in criminal behavior. They might have had poor customer service skills, and no business acumen. It's possible that their standards were so high, you considered them one of the "perfect people" and began to doubt your abilities. Eventually, retreating under the burden of imposter syndrome.

Everyone has a horror story, one they are currently living, or if they have not been able to put the nightmare to rest, they are reliving years later. It is time to move on.

It is time to write a thank you note to your lousy boss. You do not have to send it to them, but you need to invest time reframing your experience. You have a different perspective now. Like how teenagers think their parents are pretty stupid at the moment, but over time grow amazed at how much smarter they become.

Generally, your boss sees things you do not. They have more data points with which to make decisions than you do. Now, even with that knowledge, sometimes they're still idiots. In your thank you letter, think objectively and give them the benefit of the doubt.

Many times the chemistry isn't right, and you just are not destined to get along. You may grate on each other. Thank them for that. A lousy boss clarifies your dreams and values better than anyone else can. A lousy boss can motivate you into action — to find a new job, learn new skills, or try new industries, anything to get away from them.

Not to get dramatic, but to underscore an unfortunately common reality, maybe they did ruin your life. Their actions sent you down a spiral of disheartenment, uncertainty, self-loathing and despair. Write the letter and take back your agency. They may have been the trigger that put you where you are today, but today you get your power back. Express some gratitude for how far you have come and faith in where you intend to go. Use this opportunity to clarify your thoughts and set clear-cut positive goals.

Again, this is a private exercise that is meant to be cathartic. There is no need to send what you write. However, if you would like to share your insights and comments with others, so they know they are not alone that would be a terrific thing to do. I would love to read what you have learned from having a lousy boss in your life.

## *Daily Focus*

**Try The Daily Focus**
- List 10 things you need to do that will bring you closer to your goal.
- Brainstorm 10 ideas to improve a problem you're facing.
- Give 10 compliments to other people.
- List 10 things you're grateful for.

**Do this every day for a week.**
- You'll be 70 steps closer to your goal.
- You'll have 70 ideas (14 of them will be pretty good, and you just need one.)
- You'll take the focus off yourself 70 times.
- You'll find yourself surrounded in gratitude.

## *How's Your Leadership-Life Going?*

As someone who helps individuals and organizations to lead better, it is not uncommon for me to ask people, *"How's your leadership-life going?"* I get one of three responses.

**Overly Enthusiastic**
The Overly Enthusiastic are quick to respond positively. They immediately tell me about the amazing things that they are doing and how they are *"changing the world."* They often have several coaches and mentors, all of whom are transforming their lives. I am genuinely happy for these people. About half of them try to convince me to invest in something. Their enthusiasm is infectious, and sometimes it is tempting, but I know there is not a fit between us. They are fantastic and flawless, which can be entertaining to be around in small doses, but there are traces of inauthenticity. Despite their claims, they are not perfect in everything.

**Uninspired**
The Uninspired either don't respond, ignoring the question in favor of something more comfortable, like the weather, or they lack curiosity. *"I have no idea what that is?"* The concept of leading is outside their realm. That's okay; they might be fantastic individual contributors. The alarming part is when bland reactions come from established managers and leaders in an organization. They are not giving it any thought. Truthfully, it is not too shocking anymore, because it is not uncommon. Still, it is disturbing to think about the influence their position has on other people and how much energy and talent they are capable of deflating.

**Candid**
The Candid are the most satisfying to me. They share, "Some days are better than others," and then cite examples. They have a firm grasp on leadership and their shortcomings or limitations. Some pause, and are taken aback by the question. They say things like, *"No one has ever asked me that before,"* or, *"I've never thought of myself as a leader … but you know what, I am … or want to be."* People who fall into this group are fun. They are open to new perspectives, admit when they are mistaken and regularly seek out a better way of doing things that would work for them. They have humility and ambition, a couple of traits I find attractive in leaders.

When I ask someone how their leadership-life is going, I am referring to the area of their life concerning their leadership, their leadership activity on the whole, or the manner in which that person conducts themselves as a leader. I let people define what leadership-life means to them. It helps me learn more about their attitudes and beliefs about the art and discipline of leading, and about themselves.

So tell me, how is your leadership-life going?

Think Again; *Ways to Dismantle Lousy Leadership*

## *Lousy Leadership Is Easy but Expensive*

There is a prevalence of lousy leadership because it does not take too much effort to be a poor leader. There is not a huge barrier to entry for anyone who wants to become a leader. The difficulty arises when you are committed to being a "good" leader. Too many succumb to the mythology of leadership, by fulfilling their compulsion to reward leaders who demonstrably lack character, time and again. Culturally, we heap praise, more power, fame, and fortune upon those with situational ethics and a faulty moral compass. It is a shameful affliction that persists despite the visual measures of lousy leadership we witness every day.

Look for deep customer dissatisfaction, and you will find a weak leader. Scratch the surface of high employee turnover numbers and the painfully low degree of employee engagement, and you will uncover careless leadership. Attorneys may disagree, but a string of settlements become a chain of clues that shackle accountability and reveal the negligent management of problems. A plethora of lawsuits, blooming like a fresh crop, also feed on abundant fertilizer at its base.

**There is no doubt that lousy leaders are expensive. So why do good companies become complicit and keep them around?**

Hiring managers attempt to protect their ego because they do not like to admit to a poor hire decision. They hide behind process and a calendar rather than confess a lapse in judgment.

Lousy leaders often appear to be rainmakers, and money and positive cash flow is the oxygen of most companies. No one wants to be the one to cut off any streams of income, and if the organization is on life support, it is a difficult time to call out the supposed hero for misdeeds. People hate to jeopardize the lifestyle that they have become accustomed to living. This protective attribute of human nature often devolves into greed, which clouds many decisions.

There's a fair amount of cowardliness too because people do not want to engage in a confrontation. They convince themselves that the status quo isn't that bad. The situation is tolerable, and if they wish hard enough, maybe the problem will fix itself. That's rarely an effective strategy.

Maybe these companies are not as good as we would like to believe. **That is the biggest problem with lousy leaders; they diminish everything they touch, including other leaders.**

If you are a good leader but don't use your talents and skills to minimize the damage, or even unseat lousy leaders, you lessen your credibility. I am not talking about being the White Knight, that role often backfires. It takes a team to take down a lousy leader. It requires trust, a sense of stewardship, integrity to your values, and empathy for others; all things the lousy leader lacks and devalues. All these conditions make it harder to minimize the effects of poor leaders, but good leaders must not give up the fight. Lousy leaders destroy established cultures, reputable profits, and, most insidiously the careers, livelihood, and lives of those they claim to want to help. If you agree lousy leadership is expensive, go on a cost-cutting mission.

## *How Many Under Your Watch?*

If nothing else, the awareness campaign should have opened your eyes to offensive behavior. Statistics vary, but not by much.
- 1 in 3 women age 18-34 is sexually harassed at work.
- About 80% experience verbal harassment.
- Nearly 45% endure unwanted touching.
- 25% receive unsolicited lewd texts or emails.
- Nearly 20% are sexually harassed by a direct supervisor, nearly 30% from a coworker.
- Over 10% are threatened with job termination if they do not comply with the sexual request sought by the harasser.

Who are these wretched people who regularly exploit their power? Sadly, you probably know, but you, like thousands of others, lack the courage and conviction to put a stop to it. You need your job and the steady paycheck. Look the other way and don't rock the boat if you want that promotion and a flourishing career. It's not your concern anyway. It's none of your business. Best to not get involved.

Hence, the spreading of an epidemic, the sickening feeling in the pit of your stomach and the struggle to keep the rising bile at bay takes effort. It's not your life demoralized, confidence crushed, agency destroyed, or career derailed, you justify to yourself.

Is your silence worth it? Only you can answer that. Your economic situation, the direction of your moral compass, your capacity for empathy, will all steer you in a direction. It is your choice and how you choose to live with it.

Some of you though, claim to be leaders, yet you hide behind settlements and non-disclosure agreements. Your hands are tied. Not only do you blame the victim, but you also play one. You convince yourself there's nothing you can do. However, you are wrong. There are two things you could do.

Lead or leave.

If you work in a culture that allows anything close to the statistics mentioned above, and you are in a position to do something but decide not to, you have abdicated leadership, and you are a crappy person. Don't waste your time or money trying to become a better leader. I would prefer you invest it in becoming a better human being first.

For all the Harveys, Bills, and Rogers, there are thousands of more. As Warren Buffett, who was speaking about a different corporate malfeasance, once said, *"What you find is there's never just one cockroach in the kitchen when you start looking around."*

No one wants to seek them out, but we must shine a light on them and rid our houses of all manner of leader who lacks essential professionalism, decency, and integrity. Protecting them would be a significant misdirection and strategically stupid in the long run.

## *Leaders Ask*

Leaders think differently, which is one of the reasons they stand out from the crowd. Crowds tend to settle, content with how things are, or lamenting about how things were.

Leaders like comfort too, but in smaller doses. They know too much comfort leads to complacency and a false sense of certainty. They know there are at best, three certainties in life. We will all die, we will all pay taxes, and we will all face uncertainty.

Surprisingly, better leaders do not lack uncertainty. This fact does not immobilize them; it emboldens them. The tools at their disposal are no different from those anyone else can access. It has to do with their way of thinking.

They conceive possibility by asking, *If*
They discern by asking, *Which*
They weigh time by asking, *When*
They consider place by asking, *Where*
They examine the thing itself by asking, *What*
They consider motive by asking, *Why*
They study the means by asking, *How*
They think about the person or group by asking, *Who*

Did you notice? Effective leaders ask more than they tell.

When you equip yourself with these questions and are open to what they uncover, intriguing alternatives and new ways of facing old problems will emerge. If you haven't already adopted this type of thinking, you ought to consider doing so. Each day, every time you encounter uncertainty.

A word of caution, when you make a habit of thinking this way, you begin to stand out from the crowd as a leader.

## *Poor Leadership Pisses Me Off*

Throughout my management career at both Fortune 500, and regional companies, I encouraged direct reports and peers alike to stop deferring their dreams. Long a student of servant leadership, I always envisioned working in an organization that challenged and inspired those who were already good to become great. So I started one, founding my company in 2009, with the belief I could help people use their existing talents to find the aha within.

I knew then that accountability, coupled with the seemingly magical formula of vision, passion, and action could help optimistic and productive people, find creative solutions to their personal or professional problems.

I have always been troubled by the damaging effects that poor leadership, delivered either through intent or ignorance, inflicts on hardworking and well-meaning professionals. I have witnessed their mornings, filled with enthusiasm and hope, become reduced to disillusioned, disheartened and despondent husks of their former selves by late afternoon. In my career, I have experienced this from all angles. Sometimes I unwittingly subjected my direct reports to nonsensical management whim, for which I am still embarrassed. Other times, I was the unlucky recipient.

Regardless of the context, be it at work, home, in politics, or in self-management, poor leadership pisses me off. I have a visceral reaction to it. Simultaneously, lousy leadership in all its forms also inspires me to find ways to defeat it. As you may imagine, based on your own experiences in the world of which we live, this can be a stressful attitude to carry. However, I believe we have got to rout out lousy leadership wherever it roams.

When people proactively improve themselves, they also improve those they influence. Given enough time and mass, that influence can positively energize our nation and contribute to greater peace, prosperity, fun, understanding, responsibility, and liberty in the world.

I am proud that my company has been a candid resource for busy professionals who want to manage better and lead well. They have gained clarity on their purpose, values, and goals and have acquired skills that have increased their level of confidence and reduced or eliminated their instances of indecision, fear, and doubt. I operate on the assumption that people already carry the strengths they need, we just help them find the a-ha within. It is at the center of what we do.

## *Moving Your Passion Toward Excellence*

We all have a passion for something, whether it is for golf or little league; cooking or writing; acting or reading. Wine connoisseurs and bottle cap collectors abound.

What is your passion? Can you see it?
Most of you can.

What do you want to do with it? What do you envision? What do you want to accomplish?
Those are harder questions for many. Maybe you have the answers.

What are you doing? Is there determination in your eyes? Has your pulse quickened?

They say we cannot solve world hunger.
The truth is we can.

They say good things happen to those who wait.
We know the better rewards go to those who make things happen.

They said walking on the moon was a crazy idea.
They were right, but we did it anyway.

They say, "can't,"
we say, "can."

They ask, "why?"
we ask, "why not?"

They say, "if only…"
we ask, "what if…?"

They are challenged.
We challenge.

They are the passengers,
and we are the drivers.

Are you are too tired? Do you work too hard? Feel the world has been unfair? Do you frequently ask, "why me?" with a bovine expression painted across your face? Sadly, you are not alone. But, if you do know what you want; dream about it, talk about it and do it.

Look around. Working alongside you is one of the most talented people in the entire organization. They bring something that no one else does. Do you know what it is?

Find out. Learn from them. Share ideas and dreams, and once you discover what it is, what that special gift they bring to us is, tell them. Let them know you see it. Because the truth is most of them are not even aware of what they have.

Organizations grow, but do they mature? Are we enlightened enough to know what's going on and to understand where we are headed? To not only find, but also to use, the tools needed to build our future?

Some people are already there, and they are lending a hand. These are the people who do not watch the clock, but they do set the pace.

What about you? Can you be counted on?
Do your actions match your words?
Are you positive and proactive and professional in everything you say and do?
Do you create problems or do you create solutions?
Ask that person working alongside you; they will tell you.

What if they say something you don't want to hear?
What if they tell you the truth?
Thank them, wholeheartedly. Then roll up your sleeves and get to work. Learn more. Take classes; attend workshops. Find a mentor, be a mentor. Share.

Some of you think, "but I'm too busy," or "there's not enough time."

Friends, time is the great equalizer. It is one of the few man made instruments that are equally distributed in nice, easy to swallow increments. You can take 24 hours, or you can take 1,440 minutes, or 86,400 seconds. The portion is up to you. The world provides so many resources and tools to each of us.

Naysayers, smirk or gawk if you must, but while you troll and gesticulate wildly, the person next to you is learning and growing. They are developing themselves and helping others along the way; and before you know it, they will no longer be sitting beside you, because these types of people do not sit in one place for long. They know that increased learning leads to increased earning. Not just financial rewards; they earn accolades, and respect, and satisfaction.

Do you want to sit or stand? Walk or run? The decision is yours.

Reach deep inside and find out what motivates you. Set your goals. If you are tired, rest, but don't stay out of the action for too long, because as you rest, others work, and practice, and perfect their dreams. Don't be left behind.

Be leaders.
Be learners.
Be coaches.
Be students.
Be mentors.
Be mentioned.
Be proud
Be passionate.

## *Hedge Less; Lead Better*

Those who have read my work for a while know that insight frequently strikes me via the rule of threes. The first mention of something might prompt me to make a casual note. The second mention prompts familiarity and begins to breed curiosity. The third occurrence tells me it is time to take action.

One
I had lunch with a friend, and we eventually discussed the future and what we wanted in our businesses. He reminded me about the exercise of vividly visualizing my desired state. I believe in the practice and use the term, "sensual vision" with my clients. Your desired picture of success does not stop with your eyes. You should use all five of your senses to create a compelling vision. As all good friends do, he told me, "You don't always do that. Some of your words are wishy-washy." He's right, I have been slipping in some "probablys" and "kind ofs," and it's caused me to self-examine why. What am I protecting? Do I not fully believe in the goal, or myself?

Two
I met with a writer to discuss working with me on a few projects. Unsolicited, she took one of my articles and ruthlessly corrected my grammar and sentence structure. For those who enjoy fixing grammar and proper sentence structure, my writing provides fertile ground. Yes, every writer is moderately pained by editors, but I had no significant objection. She knows very little about me or my writing style, yet she removed words and made the piece stronger. I looked at the casualties, the words that fell and I saw something familiar. The "very" "sometimes" "just" and "probably" crowd.

Three
I flipped through an old spiral notebook and paused at a page where I had scratched out the title, "Nonsense Words" and listed beneath were "very," "really," "things," "was," and other usual suspects. These are also known as weasel words, and they suck the life out of your vision and goals and wreck havoc with accountability.

Weasel words lack specificity and punch. You have got to eliminate them from your writing, from your speaking, and most challenging, from your thinking whenever possible.

It's a difficult task because we use these words as a crutch. They allow us to limit or qualify our commitments with conditions or exceptions. We do so for many reasons. Mostly to protect ourselves; a helpful tool in legal and political matters, but less so everywhere else. When we use them, we are hedging, and the biggest thing we are protecting is our ego.

As leaders, particularly the new, or those embarking on something they are not yet committed to, we hedge. We want to woo followers, build a team, and we worry too much about offending. It's a concern that leaders have to get over. You will offend people, without any effort on your part and regardless of your precautions. The difference is when you have a knowing, your confidence and conviction manifest, and you are less concerned about the opinion of others because you are secure with yourself and your actions. This behavior alone will silence many detractors who don't have equal knowledge. Confidence scares those who are insecure.

Other than zealots, people don't follow leaders who are ambiguous. We appreciate sure footedness, confidence, a calming sureness in those we choose to follow. Be candid and hedge less.

Consult a list of weasel words and gradually root them out. It's not necessary to eradicate them from your vocabulary; it may not even be possible. Instead, become aware of them and look for better alternatives. Your confidence will soar, and you will lead better.

**Common weasel words in no particular order:**
A bit / A few, A little / A lot, Absolutely / Exactly, Arguably, Almost, Basically, Actually, Could, May / Might, Can / Can be, About, Many / most, Possibly, Often, Somehow / Somewhat, As much as, Fairly, Probably, Several, Really, Kind of, Usually, Rather, Just, Very, Virtually, Approximately, Awfully, Barely, Believe, But, Close to, Every, Extremely, Finally, In a sense, Like, Likely, Literally, Moderately, Nearly, Occasionally, Practically, Quite,

## *Don't Retreat*

Don't retreat. Don't let other people's patterns become your habit.

Whenever there is a tragedy that consumes our collective imaginations, we gasp and grieve. Some get pulled into news feeds and outlets, and overdose on images replayed endlessly as pundits and witnesses loop through the events until we memorize their phrases, or drown them out in tears.

Others ignore the news, defensively or intentionally. They want to protect THEIR world, from THE world.

There are the agitated, on every side of the issue, those who bellow their 'I told you so's' like crazed prophets; to either defend their opinion or reinforce their worst fears. The 'what-abouts?' who thrive with false equivalencies and attempt 'othering' the ingredients of the melting pot they do not like. The experts who breathe rarified air, proclaiming the cliched, 'unless you've walked in my shoes, you'll never know' argument. Couched as a statement of authority, but its arrogance robs the majority of us, those with differing experiences, the value of empathy.

There are the blissfully unaware; those who do not comprehend or don't care, or were away attending to other matters. Some, thankfully, are children none the wiser, their innocence preserved a while longer. For others, it is a lifestyle they fervently protect.

If your social media feed is diverse, the cadence is palatable. Well meaning quotes, old YouTube clips presented as evidence, arguments that lack nuance, or even decency. Then the call for kittens or babies, to soothe our soul and calm our nerves. Followed by the return to normalcy, or the attempt to adjust to the new normal.

These are not normal times. These times require your participation. Take a break from social media without announcing it if you must. Walk in nature without your phone if you can. Share a meal with others. Mourn in the way that's best for you.

Don't wish for things to return to how they once were because back then, things were far worse for someone you love. Instead, wish and work for a better tomorrow; for yourself and others.

Don't quit. Be fed up and take action. Practice kindness, generosity, empathy, and gratitude to get you through. Lead from where you are. Reach out and reach up.

Do not retreat because the world is scary, or dangerous, depressing, or overwhelming. Be courageous. Face the dangers and acknowledge the pain. Find a piece, a place, an act that you can do that will make a difference, even if you do not see how or where. Behave with love, kindness, and resolve. Do not retreat. We need you.

## *Do Your Direct Reports Need Leadership Coaching?*

Effective leadership coaching requires a commitment. Is it worth investing in outside resources for a direct report who is facing change or second-guessing their abilities? Here are five considerations for your decision-making matrix.

**Value** – *Are they worth it?*
Is their current performance or perceived potential, valuable to your organization? Executive coaching could become time-consuming or expensive, therefore, reserve it for high-performers.

**Challenges** – *Is there a pressing need?*
Can you pinpoint the problems they are facing right now? Some of the challenges a direct report faces may not be business related, but could still be adversely affecting performance expectations. Fundamentally, all leaders must be able to demonstrate alignment with the organization's vision, mission, and values. Leadership coaching can help regain that alignment.

**Willingness** – *Are they willing?*
Is your direct report willing to work with an outside coach? If someone on your team is not reasonably open to self-improvement, you may want to re-examine your answer to question #1.

**Alternatives** – *Can you do it?*
Have you considered alternatives to outside coaching? Better mentoring, training, or direct coaching from you, are possibilities you may want to explore before looking for an external solution.

**Support** – *Is there support?*
Are other members of your team willing to support your direct report's growth and change? Explicit or implicit negative reinforcement will neutralize any investment you make. Your office environment should bolster, not undermine, the growth of all your direct reports. If it does not, use your resources to improve your organization's culture instead.

*Note: If you answered no to three or more of the questions, you might want to consider leadership development coaching for yourself first, or perhaps in concert with your employee.*

Karl Bimshas

## *Refuse Generational Labels; You'll Lead Better*

Scroll through your social media feed, and it's highly likely you'll see a post that bashes Millennials and the generation of kids today. Usually, there's a picture of a string of teenagers looking at their phones or taking selfies with dire warnings of the coming apocalypse written underneath. Or perhaps you've seen the guilt-inducing, "share if you agree" tirade that includes a grainy vintage photo and words extolling how you came from a generation that used to play in the dirt with rusty nails, and you turned out okay.

Whether you are a part of the Lost Generation, The Baby Boomers, Generation X, Millennials, or Generation Z, is virtually meaningless for effective leaders. These labels are for broad spectrum marketing purposes, akin to arbitrarily naming storms. The World Meteorological Organization follows stringent criteria when naming hurricanes. Not so for winter storms, which The Weather Channel took upon itself to start naming in 2012 to help boost ratings. Conceivably, it helps communicate warnings, but fundamentally, it's designed to improve marketing and hype. Yes, names can help with recall later, but if you say, "The Blizzard of '78" you already have more information than "Winter Storm Maya."

Unless you are writing policy for millions of people, you shouldn't be overly concerned about generational labels. Just like with the plethora of behavior assessments, if you learn someone is a High-D, a parrot, a dolphin, or any other noun, it's simply a quick shorthand you can use to try to understand a segment of your work group. But tread lightly, because tools are only useful if the person knows how to use them. People like to fit in, to be part of a tribe, but few enjoy labels. Besides, it starts to feel arbitrary and unimportant. I anecdotally asked several people what generation they belonged to. They didn't know and had to look it up. As a general rule, resist labeling, it starts to feel a little Hesther Pryn-ish.

We like to think each generation is unique, and they are, but it's less for which Batman or James Bond they grew up with, or what national or man-made disaster they lived through, and more about which values they fit into.

Because I'm a consultant, I view the world through a quadrant matrix. There are social or personal means versus social or personal ends. Means are the methods you use, and ends are the desired goal. Social can be thought of as the whole (society), and personal is (you) or your very small

group. Social Means, tend to be concerned with the moral responsibility of the whole, while Personal Means, tend to be more concerned with individual rights. Likewise, there are Social Ends (Greatest good for the greatest number) and Personal Ends (greatest good for me.) If you break the model down to it's simplest form, it could be four sets of values.
Everybody looking out for everybody else for the greater good,
Individuals looking out for themselves for the greater good;
Individuals looking out for themselves for their good,
Everybody looking out for individual ends.

You could plug various generations into that matrix, but that would only be a snapshot, and depending on other factors, e.g. social, economic, geographic, could be potentially misleading. Generational labels, or labels of any kind, only provide a headline. To be an effective leader you need to dig into the story. That's why I believe it's more useful to look at the needs, wants, challenges and values we all share at different stages in life. Some examples:

- In our *late teens*, we are starting to get better at balancing our emotions, but we are often detached and opinionated.

- In our e*arly 20s* we think we are awesome and the world is terrible; by our late 20s we still think we're awesome, but we now think the world is what it is, and we try to figure out how we can best get along with it. We have a general ambivalence in matters of love and money. We also test our beliefs and begin to shed the ones that no longer ring true for us.

- The *early 30s* is a turning point. Those beliefs we discarded may cause conflict with our parents and other elders. Who we were is different from who we are. New things become important, and there is an urgency to "do something big" before 40.

- In *our 40s* we engage in self-assessment, and we have a renewed determination to "make it" by acquiring material things and "own it" by reclaiming a sense of agency. It is about power. It's no longer about fitting into the world. It's about creating our version of the world and contributing to it.

- By our *late 40s,* we are wondering. "is this enough?" or "Is that it?" Health-wise we often alternate between feeling like hell, and never feeling better.

- In *our 50s* things and thinking shifts, and we return to any of the unfinished business of our 30s. We go on new adventures and develop a compelling, "it's my turn" attitude.

- In *our 60s* we are filled with memories, we have a long view of circumstances and a renewed sense of urgency, and in our 70s and beyond, we have a great, if not always positive, perspective on life, are reflective and, health permitting, frequently have fun and sheer delight in the unfolding of new things.

There's no denying technology, also plays a role in defining generations; think radio, film, television, the internet. But we all share the same approximate general needs, wants, and challenges are various points in our life regardless of the enabling tools around us.

As a leader, you should be willing to test your assumptions about those who work with you. When you demonstrate curiosity and a willingness to challenge your assumptions you build empathy. Empathy, gratitude and the ability to teach are crucial skills for all leaders. It transcends generational thinking and puts greater focus on individuals. Letting them know that they matter. Spend less time budgeting for cultural perks to satisfy your team and more time exploring the strengths of those who are willing to help you achieve your vision, regardless of generation.

## *Adapt Your Style*

There are writers who have a particular style, and there are writers who can adapt their styles to different needs.

There are leaders who have a particular style, and there are leaders who can adapt their styles to different needs.

There's not a right or wrong; there's good and better.

## *For Leaders who Cringe on Sundays*

Well-meaning managers and leaders fail to find the time to recharge because you know you could be managing better.
It is not imposter syndrome. It is because you have left something unresolved and allowed it to fester over the weekend, if not over several weekends. That's a problem because you have probably robbed yourself of valuable time to refresh and you are likely to start the new week with a chip on your shoulder.

Not a smart path toward success.

If this sounds familiar, I'd like to help make the problem go away for you. Identify the "biggest thing" that you left unresolved last week. You intuitively know what it is. Maybe you'll have to go back a few weeks to pinpoint it.

Make the resolution of that problem your priority. Not '*a*' priority. '*The*' priority. If you have multiple priorities, you are using the word wrong. You may not be able to resolve the issue in a day or a week. Although, you might be able to with one phone call or an empathic meeting. It is amazing what you can accomplish when you do what you've avoided. The point is to take action and keep taking action with the intent to arrive at a resolution.

A word or caution. You may not be satisfied with the resolution. The answer may not go your way. Perhaps you lose. Yes, that will suck, but a loss is better than abdicating.
Lead.

## *Don't Listen to Them; You're Fine*

People make a lot of money off your lack of self-esteem or self-awareness. You're not good looking enough, your car is too wimpy or guzzles too much fuel. Your teeth could be whiter, your family happier, your waist thinner, and if you want to trust cartoon bears, your butt could be cleaner. You are stupid for whom you voted for; your job lacks pizzazz, in fact, your whole career could be better if you went to the right college. Not the one that costs too much, or the one that lacks prestige, the other one. The team you root for is great, but not the greatest, and your kids would be smarter if they wore high-performance shoes. You could find the perfect partner if you were more assertive, but didn't talk as much. The food you are feeding your family is probably killing them, and if you cared you would protest, but not with those people, they are all idiots. Just do seven things for 10,000 hours, or is it 10,000 things for seven hours? Doesn't matter, to be exceptionally successful you only need four hours, essential oils, a protein shake and the right selfie, which you should pay an expert to take for you.

Exhausted yet? Low energy, no stamina. Sad.

It seems impossible to do it all; to be all things to all people. You cannot. You should not. Don't listen to them; you're fine.

Knowing there are more than 300 million people affected by depression worldwide won't keep you from feeling alone, and the fact that 18% of the U.S. population experiences some type of anxiety disorder brings no comfort. Clearly, we need a better system to filter what informs our outlook and influences our decisions. Lousy leaders prey on those with learned helplessness and hopelessness. Stop feeding lousy leaders, starve them off.

Clear the thorns and weeds that are cluttering your personal path and define success for yourself on your terms. Spend a few moments to quiet the sounds competing for your attention. Then prune the excesses in your life, material or otherwise, and capture your answers to the following questions.

1. What problem do you want a hand in solving? (Vision)
2. Why? (Passion)
3. What step can you take in the next five seconds, minutes or hours to inch closer to solving that problem? (Action)
4. Repeat. (Consistency and Discipline)

These four steps are just as easy to complete as they are to ignore. You get to select which path to take. If you choose to equip yourself with self-directed vision, passion, action, consistency and discipline, you will fare better.

## *Writing Letters to Your Younger Self*

It is all the rage, particularly during graduation season, for well-meaning self-help gurus to encourage you to write a letter to your younger self. Invariably to find words of wisdom accumulated through years of experience which support the phrase, *"If I only knew then what I knew now."*

Newsflash: You didn't.

Don't dwell on it. None of your early knowledge will be better than your later experience. Right now, you have a set of values, a vision, and a mission that is important to you. You know where you want to go. You don't have all the answers, but you already have a 'true north' you check in with to keep you on track, and just as importantly, you have enthusiasm. These positive feelings and behaviors have a tendency to wither over time and transform into regret. That's why penning a letter to your younger self is so often recommended. It's a way for you to get back in touch with your 'inner child' and extol a kind of parental wisdom on yourself.

I say, screw that. That's frequently the problem with leadership autobiographies. The author whitewashes bad decisions and sacrifices perspective on the journey to make themselves look better on the outside and feel better on the inside. It is revisionist and helps no one.

To proactively defeat this problem you would be better served writing a letter to your future self. I don't care if you are still in high school, graduating college, in your 40s, 60s or 80s. You, today, are your future younger self. Use the opportunity to speak some truth to power. You will change, some for the better, some perhaps, for the worse, in the next three to five years. Yell out to your future self, a reminder of what you stand for and want to accomplish. Write what you think will be important for you to know, believe, and hold dear while allowing room for growth and adaptability.

This letter will serve as your wake-up call two, three, or five years down the road. You may find what you write becomes your code of conduct, the behaviors you want to retain and be living by if you want your goals to have any merit or fulfillment. Archive your letter and set a date to open it in a few years. You will find it refreshing to learn how true to your younger self you have stayed. Or, if you face melancholy, you can decide to make a change and write a new letter. It's your life and your choice. Any change you make will come in the future, not in the past.

## Basketball Players, Filmmakers, and Nurses

Ask a basketball player about the game, and they will talk about possessions of the ball, the clock, openings they created, and specific shots they took. Of course, winning is, important, but the great ones know they get there shot by shot.

Filmmakers will often put themselves in precarious positions and often go to extraordinary lengths to capture the right moment in the frame. Sometimes oblivious to their surroundings, other times, uniquely aware, yet they always remain focused. They take great pride in getting the shot.

Ever contend with a frightened toddler just before for their annual immunization? Nurses deal with squirming, emotional, flailing children every day. They do not have the luxury of waiting until the tyke has stoically calmed down. The good ones know how to create the right environment, where they can swoop in, and seemingly effortlessly if not painlessly, give the shot.

Professionals in these diverse fields know how to manage time, look for or create opportunities, and get the shot in. Sometimes they miss, but when they do, they don't crumble to the floor and soak their sorrows with a pint of ice cream. They brush off their failed attempt and keep at it until they get it right. Then they celebrate with a first bump, a high-five, a little wink and a sticker, not with a parade down city boulevards. They all know that it is the shot, although small, brief, and not award-winning in and of itself, that always serves the greater mission. To win the game, tell the story, protect the child.

**The great ones, practice and perfect the routine.**

What about you? Are your everyday actions serving your greater purpose? You do not accomplish your purpose without first stringing together many, much smaller and repetitive steps over time.

- Manage your time.
- Look for and make opportunities.
- Get your shot in.
- Celebrate briefly.
- Go on to the next one.

## How's Your Customer Love Life?

Do you think your customers are infatuated with you, or are you delusional?

Reminder, your client, is the person, or persons, who decide to do business with you and your organization. You have internal and external customers. Your external customers usually have more choices than your internal ones, and they are driven to pick the service, product, or solution that provides the best value. Some, sometimes many, choose you. Repeatedly.
How do you show them your appreciation?

*Do you love your clients?*
Do they know? Have you explicitly told them? More importantly, have you shown them? Words are cheap. Intention is nice; action is better.

*Can your clients count on you when they need you?*
Do they count on you? Do they need you? Really?

*Are you quick to help your clients?*
Do you offer suggestions or solutions that benefit them even if the best solution doesn't benefit you?

*Are you easy to do business with?*
Are you and your team happy to greet your clients, or do you make them feel like they are an imposition to your work?

*Do your clients trust you?*
How do you know? Do you trust them?

*Do you provide your clients with solutions that fit their needs at the right price?*

Be honest, have you ever felt over appreciated? I doubt it. Everyone could stand to feel more admiration and respect. Start with your clients, both internal and external. Show them some love. Today is a great day to start.

## *4 Time Chunks for Better Performance*

To be more productive in your life start organizing your major activities into four areas.

**Prepare**
Do the prep work. Invest time in the practice and learning required to meet your specific performance needs. Pick the formula and ratio that works for you. Example: Allot four hours of practice and preparation for every one hour of performance. That might seem extreme, but it could be too little for you. Consider the effort professional athletes put in toward their daily practice. A four to one ratio may be your sweet spot for success. The minimum would be one to one. Yes, that means if you run a weekly one-hour meeting, you are also investing one hour for planning (agenda, presentation, objection handling, etc.) Adopting this discipline forces you to deeply consider the content and context of your meetings and other high-stake performances.

**Perform**
Showtime. The well-known often maligned Pareto Principle, states that 80% of results come from 20% of activity. The activities to focus on are your key money making activities. The biggest, high leverage skills required for you to get the largest return on your investment of time, treasure, or talent. Because, your performance is what others count on, come to see, and is what you are judged on.

**Review**
Many people skip this altogether. Bad move. The time you make in this phase will vary depending on the importance of the activity. In some instances, it may be as long as the prep work or the length of the performance. Minimally, make it half the length of the performance, until you refine your process. The review phase is simply a "facts only" after action review of what happened, what worked or didn't, and what to do differently the next time around. Doing this puts closure to the performance, so you don't drag regrets forward, nor rest on your laurels.

**Rejuvenate**
The ability to take necessary downtime and use it wisely is a strategic advantage many people fail to employ. This period is where you pursue other interests, play, relax and otherwise recover. People think of this as vacation time. It is more than that. Rest is required for other parts of your mind to be activated. If your performance was technical in nature, this might be a more artistic time for you. Have you ever felt exhausted yet restless binge watching old movies? It is your mind's way of telling you that particular low-grade activity isn't cutting it, and it is searching for fresh inputs for rejuvenation. You would do well to help it along.

Let your current priority decide which phase to schedule first. If you are always stressed and not making enough time for yourself, schedule rejuvenation time right away. If you have completed a time tracking study of your day or week, and you know what the significant activities are, schedule those first, and then backfill the prep time, and allow for a review period.

**Prepare. Perform. Review. Rejuvenate. Repeat.**
Essentially it is a formula you need to solve based on your priorities. Once you figure out the schedule that best works for you, honor it and begin to enjoy greater results and productivity.

## Are You an Authoritarian at Work?

Lousy Leadership Hidden in Hubris

Leadership, like water, is not inherently good or bad, but it is essential. The desire for water changes depending on the conditions. Those parched in the desert are desperate for a sip of anything, while those battling floods pray for torrential rain to abate. Some are afraid of swimming or getting wet, and others frolic amongst the waves. Water can be sweetened or poisoned. It can appear frozen and inaccessible, scalding hot, or be as ephemeral as fog. It can be used to torture or nourish. How we view water and how we view leadership can vary widely.

It is important to know which style of leadership is most useful in a given situation. Far too many people do not recognize differences, and a greater number disempower themselves by not challenging corrosive leadership early on. They sip the water, and may think it tastes a little funny, but merely shrug and assume someone else will take care of it. That in itself is lousy leadership. Even a content individual contributor should feel compelled to rise and challenge notions that interfere with core values and common purpose. Poor leadership practices are not reserved for politicians. They are present in boardrooms, showrooms, shop floors and kitchens around the globe.

Each environment changes based on the knowledge and willingness of those being lead, be they employees, customers, investors, or citizens. Those who are frightened by their perceived threat of "outside forces," tend to like strong authority figures. It is a proxy for the comfort they feel from a big blanket wrapped around them, a deadbolt on the door, or a gun under the bed. When people do not know what to do, they like to be told what to do. This is where the authoritarian begins, under the guise of keeping followers safe from them, the outside forces. In business, you may convince yourself those enemy forces are the competition or government regulation. While At home, it could be the neighbors across the street who have a different complexion or cook food that smells unpleasant to you.

Businesses do not have to be democracies, and many are not. Often, when stakes are high, they can become dictatorial. A few reassuring nods of agreement from the leader's staff and followers is all it takes for the authoritarian style to begin.

Are you inadvertently fulfilling the predictable steps of an authoritarian dance with your workplace behavior?

**Step one:**
Do you believe all outside information sources are suspect, that everyone has self-serving agendas, and only you can properly educate your followers, your employees, clients, investors? They should only accept the information you share as being true because you have the greatest knowledge and you are the only one who can keep them safe from harm, e.g. unemployment, layoffs, poor investments. You implore others never to trust the grapevine filled with rumor and innuendo. (Aka, 'blame the media.')

**Step two:**
Have you ever uttered the phrase, "You are either with us, or you are against us" to members of your team? Do you consider exploratory interviews with the competition acts of disloyalty? Have you expressed explicitly or implicitly that any opposition to your ideas makes others traitorous in your eyes? You publicly or privately smear and punish others by questioning their loyalty to the team or company, and accuse them of letting outside threats into the organization. Have you called anyone who has reservations about your ideas and actions, traitors?

**Step three:**
Do you oppose ideas and notions that others bring from outside information sources? Do you try to convince those who disagree with you that their judgment is clouded and they are not thinking straight? You say their ideas are dangerous and could easily multiply and spread, like cancer. You could use other metaphors like virus, bacteria, or pollen, but nothing elicits fear, disgust, and a lack of agency like cancer. You think that description fits best.

**Step four:**
To convince holdouts that the nonsense they keep spewing is falling on deaf ears, have you hastily organized morale-boosting meetings, with attendance mandatory and actual crowd size exaggerated? You point to these large gatherings with participants awash in a sea of company colors and forced enthusiasm, as 'social proof' of your success.

**Step five:**
For you, most of this has been fun, even exhilarating. You and your lieutenants have successfully laughed off and diminished your critics. Your

followers, who once felt fearful are buoyed and emboldened by an apparent safety in numbers. Hubris strikes hard, and the smartest people in the room go dumb because they have disconnected themselves from alternative points of view. In this stage, you find ways to the change well-established rules, policies, mores, and practices, to better benefit you personally, or to demonstrate your perceived power with acts of whim. Your defense nearly always starts by arguing the letter or the law, not the spirit of the law (see Enron). At this stage, the evidence is confirmed that your primary concern as the leader is not in those you serve, but in your individual interests first and foremost. In governing bodies, personal freedoms in the name of security, are reduced faster and faster.

Soon the dance is over, and any leadership style valuing democratic virtues are left breathless.

Authoritarian-like leadership can be useful in a dramatic, short-lived crisis, where there is no time to debate or consider alternatives. However, it should never be a way of life, nor a way to run a business, family, or country. Remember, a strong leader at any level can take criticism, and will often invite it so that they can make a well-informed, deeply considered decision. Despite the bravado and often ruthless appearance, authoritarian leaders are inhabited by weak, frightened people.

To be an effective leader, never succumb to the temptation of using authority as your go-to tool. It deadens your empathy and hastens the demise of the organization and people that support you.

## *Guard the Gate*

Not long ago we didn't give too much thought about where we got our information. Primarily it was filtered through our family and friends. There were other filters in place. Our schools had a set of standards, depending on where you lived. Our newspapers and television programs had a point of view. Even the local bookstore decided which authors and magazines to stock on the shelves.

It would be a mistake to think those filters no longer exist. What has changed is we have far more control and access to "inputs" than we ever have had before, but to many, it all comes through as indiscernible noise.

Start segmenting all your inputs to regain some order. Newspapers have sections; the front page, national, international, local, entertainment, food, science, education, etc. Editors put related stories in each section. When they blur the lines and place a science story in the entertainment section, it causes confusion, miscommunication, and ire.

Watch or listen to any news program for a while, and you recognize they have blocks designated between commercial breaks. Leading with a quirky human interest story and then burying the news of the day somewhere in the middle makes no sense and would rapidly lose the audience.

Yet, regular confusion, miscommunication, and ire are what many people allow to wash over them with un-curated social media. They accept streams polluted with a nauseating mix of adorable kitten videos adjacent to war atrocities. Birth announcements from old classmates juxtaposed with tasteless jokes, slacktivism pleas, and business proposals. How to make fat-free guacamole wins attention over images of suffering refugees, and a tweetstorm on the audacity of some establishment not carrying a size six Jimmy Choo can easily drown everything else for a few hours.

This chaos warps the brain and causes people to retreat into separate camps for reassurance. They range from those who abdicate responsibility, to those who take every hangnail as an assault against civilization. Perhaps you rest somewhere between the two?

How can you solve this?

Don't rely on, nor wait for, a company or a government to be your gatekeeper. Take the initiative and begin compartmentalizing your social media feeds, and friends, and any other information input sources. Think like a newspaper; anticipate the sections of interest and categorize accordingly. Do you want only headlines? Which topics deserve deeper analysis? What do you need to learn more about? Are you open to views that oppose your own? Do you want your beliefs and perspective challenged, affirmed, or both? How much time will you devote to entertainment and diversions?

Begin to use the various social and other media channels, for different purposes. Don't let one entity become your default screen.
If you are not sure how to organize the many inputs of your life, consider starting with these four sections.

- **Briefing** – What information will help you prepare for what's to come?

- **Tools** – What information will help you better execute your tasks today?

- **Analysis** – What information will help you evaluate what you have accomplished and what you need to consider going forward?

- **Recreation** – What information will help you recharge and perhaps be open to new challenges?

Build your personal intelligence gathering system around those categories to start.

It is possible, even crucial, to allow space for happenstance and serendipity in your life, while taming the unrelenting onslaught of unfiltered pandemonium that clamors for attention. Start today. You will be more productive and less susceptible to dangerous distractions tomorrow.

## Run an After Action Review for Your Year

It is now the season when countless articles on how to plan your year pop up like premature Crocus. These systems will ask you to dig deep and often provide a daunting number of exercises designed to make you think, dream, pray, meditate or vision board your new year.

Presumably, you have planned your year before, and maybe even have a preferred method. You can go through any planning gyration you feel comfortable with, but until you properly close out one year, you are not going to make much progress in the next. Because without active learning, you will be prone to making the same mistakes you have always been making and habitually falling into the same patterns.

Before you begin your new year, make a note of the lessons you learned in this one. Spend a few moments conducting an after action review.

Many people dread looking back, particularly if it has been a tough year, but answering a few questions will help prepare you so you can have a better year. If you are naturally introspective, review the following questions while sitting with a cup of coffee. If you are naturally social, you might want to get with good friends and interview each other. Make a fun event out of it. Have dinner or brunch at home and use the questions as topics of discussion. Make notes from your appetizers all the way through dessert. It is a productive use of time with loved ones in these waning days of the year.

**After Action Review**

- What was your objective this year? – *What did you set out to do, or want to accomplish?*

- What happened? – *Provide just the facts, no opinions.*

- What worked? – *Why? Knowing why will help you replicate it in the new year.*

- What do you need to do more of? – *Why? What could you put more resources toward?*

- What didn't work? – *Why?*

- What do you need to change about your approach or goals going forward? – *Why? You may have had a good idea, but poor execution.*

- Who needs to be recognized for aiding you your progress? – *Someone has helped you along the way. Make a plan to thank them appropriately.*

- What are you most proud of this year?

- What do you regret doing this year? *It likely started with something you said.*

- What do you regret not doing this? *This regret often stings the most.*

- As of today, how satisfied (Very Dissatisfied / Dissatisfied / Ambivalent / Satisfied / Very Satisfied) are you with the following areas of your life?

    o Career?
    o Contribution?
    o Education?
    o Finances?
    o Health?
    o Recreation?
    o Relationships?
    o Personal?

- What will you cease? – *Think about one or two of the biggest things you know you have to stop doing if you want to increase your effectiveness. It is likely a bad habit or attitude which you will need to change.*

- What will you commence? – *Determine which new habits, attitudes, or actions you will need to adopt and demonstrate that are most likely to boost your effectiveness. You may have avoided these in the past. It is time to try them this year.*

- What will you continue? – *You are doing some things right. What are your "winning ways" and how will you ensure you keep doing them despite any distractions that may arise?*

After you review your answers, it will be easier to create three main goals for the new year. For each goal, determine how much (*a unit measure*) and by when (*a time measure*) and then decide on the next action you need to complete to move you closer.

Investing the time in an after action review for the year, or any valuable project, helps you learn faster and improves your performance. Use it for any area of your life including your personal and professional leadership. Doing so will help you manage better and lead well.

## *Your Year Was Not Great*

Your year was not great. The majority of the people you know didn't have a great year either. How can that be?

Most people start the year filled with hope and optimism. Great attributes, but a poor substitute for persistence and pragmatism. People *wish* for a happy new year, but they seldom put in the *effort* necessary for a happy new year.

This time of year is a lot like changing trains at a busy station. We rush out of our compartments and spill out onto the platform, ladened with our accumulated luggage. Some travelers have been here before, and they seem to know where to make their connection, but many get overwhelmed by the streams of people coming from all directions at different velocities.

The observant will notice some passengers have no bags, while others rely on a porter. There are groupings of individuals, couples, families; young and old. Some stumble across old friends, get distracted and are happy to catch a later train. Others, rudely plow through the crowds, leaving an undulating path in their wake.

Whistles blow, announcements are made, and we all run to our desired train, hoping this one will get us closer to our destination. A few, blindly board the nearest locomotive. In some cases, it is the one they had just disembarked. They want to return from whence they came; others are in an oblivious rut.

Regardless of your circumstance, pack appropriately for your trip. Your values, your purpose (if you have one) and your integrity, are a few of the essentials to carry with you.

Always try to lighten your load. Don't bring your baggage of worries, and know ahead of time what train you want to get on. Control what you can. Recognize that you are on the right track. Then let go and stay productive during the trip.

If you are pursuing wanderlust, the destination of the train will not matter, though even then, you were probably choosy about the general direction you wanted to take.

If you are committed to pursuing a worthwhile goal, make a plan and then work that plan. Give yourself permission to allow for adjustments along the way. There will be delays, disruptive travel companions, perhaps questionable food choices. Your view will not always be spectacular, contingent on which side of the train you sit. Others may find a beautiful vista to be a burdensome distraction. Choose wisely.
Either way, have safe journeys and enjoy the ride.

## Decide with SPICE

When your task list becomes too long and neglected and reads like a list of forgotten dreams, or you are regularly swamped with new ideas, resist the urge to dabble. Dabbling in a few things will only dilute your focus and energy.

So, how do you choose which projects to take on? Going with your gut is okay for some things, but as humans, we tend to grossly overestimate (men) or underestimate (women) our capabilities. It turns out; we are not as objective as we like to think.

Using a tool to provide some objectivity and focus on the tasks and great ideas you are drowning yourself in will help.

Add a little spice.

Here are five criteria you can use to filter the worthiness of your ideas. Use a numeric scale, 0-4 for example, to rate the low and high probability of each element for every project you are considering.

**S.P.I.C.E.**

**Speed**. How quickly can you implement this task or idea?

**Profitable**. How profitable with this task or idea be to your bottom line or important relationships?

**Impact**. How much impact will finishing this task or idea have on your greater goals and values?

**Client-focused**. How closely associated with delivering excellence to your client is this task or idea?

**Ease**. How easy, relative to everything else on your plate, is this task or idea to accomplish?

You could weigh the criteria that are more relevant to your situation, but there will always be some subjectivity when answering these questions. By and large running your big ideas or daily to-dos through this lens will clearly define what is best to focus your energy and attention upon.

## *Your Leadership Agenda*

Your attitude, your appearance, and your approach are the three building blocks of your leadership agenda.

Your leadership agenda is how you plan on guiding your organization in the coming months. "Organization" can be your family, your department, your company, your squad, your bowling league, any entity you are part of leading and trying to take someplace different from where you are today.

Your leadership agenda could focus on the next thirty days or the next six months. I find 90 days to be a reasonable timeframe.

The core of your agenda includes a collaborative relationship between your attitude, appearance, and approach.

Your **attitude** is your *inner game*. The belief system you carry with you. It is your personal compass that points to things like your purpose, values, and goals. It is also where you find your leadership philosophy.

Your **appearance** is your *outer game*. It is how you show up and present yourself as a leader. This doesn't have to mean a top of the line suit and nice shoes, although it could. It means dressing and acting the part. A hoodie and jeans, or top hat and tails, neither matters. The leader stands out, sometimes by a lot, sometimes subtly, but they are always recognizable to those they lead. It is how you carry yourself physically, your body language, your method of communication, and your attire.

Your **approach** is your *behavior* and how you treat others. In many ways, it is the manifestation of your attitude and your appearance. When all things are congruent, your leadership appears effortless, even when it's not. When there is a disconnect, you look haphazard.

The idea behind your leadership agenda is to pick the most important item in each category that you want to emphasize or improve over the next 90 days so you can more successfully lead your organization forward.

I use a systematic process to help busy professionals determine each element, but the quick hack follows.

- Your **attitude** is either a strength you have or a disciplined thought process you want to incorporate.

- Your **appearance** is a physical representation of your leadership that most aids your cause.

- Your **approach** is a particular behavior most likely identified by a dispassionate assessment like DISC or a Leadership360 which you want to enhance or improve to better your results.

These three elements are always part of the essential leadership skills you need to be a successful leader. By giving them focus for 90 days, you begin to embed them into your ongoing leadership style.

## *Remember Context*

When you stop to think about an interaction with someone or a group of people, it is easy to reflect on three components.

1. You.
2. Them.
3. Your conversation with them.

Rudimentary, yet you probably don't think about it too much, except when you are retelling the story of what happened (or didn't happen,) to a third party.

Start giving these three components greater thought before your interaction, and you will come across more professional.

The fourth component is nearly always missed, except by exceptional leaders.

Context.

Knowing what has happened recently, or being aware enough to see what's occurring presently, often makes all the difference between a pleasant conversation and an argument.

Seek to know what's going on with the people you communicating with so you can improve your message and get better results.

## *Focus Can Be Difficult*

Focus can be difficult. There are so many welcome and unwelcome distractions in our world.

If you don't know your vision, purpose, and values, the challenge is even greater.

Start defining them so your decision-making can get easier.

Next list an immediate goal, a short-term goal, and a long-term goal.

Do something each day that supports those goals and keeps you aligned with your vision, purpose, and values.

It's not easy. It does get easier.

## *Organize Your Thoughts*

Some people are great at creating lists. They have impressive lists. Accomplishing tasks, a little less so.

Some people are decisive and action oriented. They get lots of things done fast, and then they redo a lot of things faster.

Some people think … and think … and think.
Others, seem to put very little thought into what they do.

People have different styles, and strengths. It is what makes the world go 'round.

Experiment and find a system that works for you.

Capture ideas. Decide which ones support your immediate goals and which ones you want to save for later. Know when to cross items out, or delete them.

Discover your strengths, and shortcomings, and resources to help with both.

Figure out, "How much and by when?" for every action.

Thoughts are great, but meaningless without action.

Actions without context create more confusion than clarity.

Leaders create clarity and take action.

## *Decide How You are Going to Lead*

A good number of leadership problems I see come about because the leader has never given any thought to the question, "How are you going to lead?"

Many are dumbfounded. Though to be fair, if you ask a writer, "How are you going to write?" there is similar confusion.

The smart ones in both camps reply with a smile and say, "Well."

That's a good start. No one aspires to be a lousy writer or a lousy leader, yet both are abundant.

After some thought, a writer might talk about their discipline. "I will write for three hours every night and edit four hours during the day." They might talk about outlines, research, summoning the muse. They envision book launches, cocktail parties, and movie adaptations.

As heart-quickening and aspirational as all that may be, it still leaves the question unanswered.

Given enough time to ponder, the writer will talk about other authors, the books they like and abhor, favorite characters, settings, styles, and genres. They talk about their craft and how they are working to improve it. What rules they adhere to, which ones they bend, and those they detest and ignore. They have opinions and a point of view. They have a preferred method of writing but will use charcoal bricks on a brick wall to capture their words if they must.

What they have is a philosophy.

So should a leader. You ought to have a plan as to how you will lead, yet have flexibility if conditions change. What other leaders do you learn from, positively and negatively? What do you like about leading, what makes you uncomfortable? What kind of people and causes do you easily support, what challenges you? What norms and perspectives do you honor, and which ones do you rebel against? How do your strengths and values inform your point of view? Is it unyielding, or will it change if you suddenly work for a competitor?

You may not have answers, but you should be curious enough to start finding out. Learn more about yourself, so your leadership is decisive and confident, based on your purpose, not on a whim.

## *Don't Imitate*

When you are leading well, you constantly look for what can give you and your team an edge on results while supporting your mission, vision, and values.

You could search for someone who is successful in an area you want greater improvement in, and try to replicate what they did to get there. The biggest problem with that strategy is, you are not them; you're someone different. You have a different perspective, work ethic, values, constraints, and mental head trash that is unique to you. It is a better use of time to learn what ideas they tried and failed at, so you can be prepared to navigate the inevitable difficulties you will face.

When you imitate what successful people do, you will not stand out. That may be okay if your goal is to blend in. However, those who want to make a bigger impact also take a look at the opposite of what has happened or is currently being done, offered or supplied. They know that these are the neglected areas. Now, they may very well be neglected for valid reasons, but you may uncover a new way to address an unmet need that everyone else is ignoring and that could make a dramatic difference.

## *Leadership Maintenance*

Now and then you need to take a look under the leadership hood and make sure things are running well.

Start by inspecting your biggest goal. Run a self-diagnosis of six systems:

1. **Your Operating Principle** – What you are trying to achieve?
2. **Your Values and Strengths** – Are they aligned and do they support your goal?
3. **Goal Articulation** – Do you know what you are trying to accomplish and can you easily explain it to others?
4. **Key Actions** – What do you physically need to do to move forward?
5. **Success Metrics** – How do you know if you are "winning" or "losing"?
6. **Resources** – Who or what could help you with any element of your goal?

Next, assess how well you are performing with your essential leadership skills. What are those? The short answer, it depends on your organization, culture, team, and what you want to achieve. Broadly identified, these are the skills that if you don't use them, you will often be prevented promotion, get reprimanded, or otherwise derail your career. Some people call these "soft skills," but given the consequences of failing to employ them, that seems disingenuous.

I cluster **Essential Leadership Skills** around five key areas:

1. **Communication, Influence & Persuasion** – How well do you listen and communicate ideas and actions with others?
2. **Management, Strategy, and Results** – How well do you incorporate your management skills with creating and supporting larger strategies that achieve your desired results?
3. **Situational and Interpersonal Awareness** – How easily do you assess the motivations, skills, barriers and distractions of others and

appropriately respond?
4. **Creativity and Problem-solving** – How adaptable, flexible and persistent are you and are those traits contagious?
5. **Professional Acumen and Attitude** – How much respect and dignity do you provide and earn through your regular interactions?

Most of your career blind spots come from these five areas. Many people who are individual contributors do not know that they exist. For others, problems occur when they ignore their shortcomings in one or more skill set.

Periodically checking your leadership systems and running some preventative maintenance will increase the mileage you get from your career.

## *Expect the Best, Plan for the Worst*

While I was growing up, I often heard the popular refrain, *"Expect the best and plan for the worst."* I attributed it to the weather. In New England, you might plan a nice picnic, but if you were smart, you also prepared a contingency for rain, or sometimes, just as likely, snow.

When I moved to the west coast, the sentiment began to fade into the California haze. How could you possibly imagine rain would have the audacity to show up and ruin an otherwise idyllic day? On the rare occasion, rain does come unexpectedly; you can see a wave of angst wash over the population of those who did not plan for the worst.

The adage is a touch flippant; along the lines of, *"trust but verify."* It makes sense, even though the act of verifying trust pretty much dissolves the trust, at least for one side of a relationship. *"Expect the best, plan for the worst,"* can make an optimist cringe and a pessimist chuckle. That's okay because it's designed for the pragmatist.

We know that positive expectations more often than not produce positive results. While wishing alone does not make it so, keeping your standards high and working to achieve them, often does. Planning for the worst doesn't make you negative; it makes you prepared.

Things very rarely unfold exactly as we plan. There are constantly other seen and unseen factors buffeting against our objective. Why this constantly surprises us is a regular source of amusement for me. Challenges are inevitable. When you plan for the worst, you increase your adaptability. You learn more about what antagonizes you and have ways to parry whatever life throws at you. That is what you want in a leader and should practice on yourself. Dream big, and imagine the means to combat setbacks, so you can make them a reality.

## *Lousy Leadership is Scary*

Lousy leadership is scary because it is so prevalent in our lives, and no one is fully immune from it. New and established managers both make errors because of impatience, or fear, or poor judgment. These mistakes frequently most hurt the people being lead. A good leader acknowledges their faults, makes corrections, and tries to make amends. A good leader is devoted to continual learning, not only for process improvements, and people development; they also look for ways to better themselves.

What makes lousy leaders scary is, through intent or ignorance, they do not look at self-improvement. They don't recognize their shortfalls, and if they carelessly harm the relationship of a customer or a direct report, they shrug it off, or worse, pass blame.

Being technically proficient in the skills of your chosen industry is great, and something everyone should aim toward. Accomplishing that alone does not make you a leader, even if someone decides to promote you to a title that seems to confer leadership status. That is more likely a case of 8s promoting 7s. It is mismanagement, and another example of why lousy leadership is hard to eradicate.

Leadership skills, like writing skills, are about influence. Their job is to make the unseen, seeable; to convey knowledge to the unknown. To cause excitement in the curious, not to incite the discontented. It entails nuanced relationship skills; reading people and being brave and bold enough to challenge wrongs. It involves the acumen to run productive meetings, garner relevant resources, and knowing when to change course and when to plow forward.

Seldom learned in a classroom and lecture hall, these skills are learned on the playgrounds, and in the walks between places with friends. They are learned while camping, or negotiating dinner and a movie. Yes, they can be found in books but must be actively uncovered with highlighters and reflected upon in journals or through discussions over coffee. The study of leadership is not a passive endeavor.

Start with you. Test your assumptions. You are wrong more than you care to admit. That's okay. It is a shared human trait. Refuse to accept axioms on blind faith. Make a note of your findings, and adjust.

What scares me is, we tolerate lousy leadership in others, and in ourselves. Blame it on constant negative reinforcement, the decay of trust, the suspicion of those who differ in thought, faith, color or cell phone choice. Our biases grow and will continue to unless we challenge them. Tear off masks that impede promises of transparency, but don't gloat. Reconcile. Recalibrate. Learn. Constantly. Otherwise, we will be haunted by lousy leadership.

## *You Goofed. Now What?*

Candidly, you won't see this properly demonstrated by people in the public eye too often. On the other hand, exceptional leaders know how, when, and why to apologize. Follow the six steps below to stand out as a better leader who shows respect and understands the meaning of the word.

**1. Admit you have done something wrong, and you need to make up for it.**

"Never apologize and never explain--it's a sign of weakness," was uttered by John Wayne in an old western. Great screenwriting, perhaps, but lousy leadership advice. Hang up your spurs, cowboy, because one; you are no John Wayne. Second, that kind of faux machismo might play well with a sliver of certain crowds; it is nowhere near as effective as the people who follow it like to believe.

**2. Take full responsibility for your actions and sincerely apologize to anyone you have harmed.**

Own it. Always. Don't waste energy and credibility looking for a scapegoat. You are 100% responsible for your actions. Don't take pride in harming fellow human beings. Take time to acknowledge your actions, even if inadvertent, have hurt them.

**3. Apologize with urgency.**

An apology does not get better with anticipation. It is not some secret gift you bestow upon someone. Don't wait for the lawyers or your advisors to craft a weak, self-protecting mia culpa. Once you know you blew it, fix it. After you apologize, you can let the lawyers and advisors do their work and help make your intentions better.

**4. Tell anyone you have harmed specifically what you did wrong and how you feel about what you did.**

You know what you did wrong, they know what you did wrong, but that's not enough to get you off the hook. You have to prove you know what you did wrong and let them validate your conclusion. Sharing how you feel illustrates your sincerity and humanity.

**5. Recognize that what you did is inconsistent with whom you want to be.**

You likely didn't intentionally mess up, it was not your goal when you work up, but it happened. It's a setback in your quest for perfection, or acting like the person you have said you want to be. That's one reason why your mistake should be equally upsetting to you.

**6. Make amends and demonstrate your commitment to not repeat the act by changing your behavior.**

Find a way to "make them whole" again. You probably won't be able to, but that should not stop you from trying to find ways to compensate for your actions and visible change your behavior going forward to prove you are serious.

You can choose to do nothing. Cling to outdated beliefs that being sorry is being weak, and you will blend in with everyone else. Maybe that will make you feel better. However, if you are a leader you know it is not about you.

Ultimately it is up to others to decide whether or not to accept your apology. Go about asking for it correctly, and the chances are better that they will, and you will earn a reputation as a stronger leader.

## *No, Your Customers Don't All Love You*

Whenever I hear an entrepreneur or executive describe how much their customers love them, I cringe. I am reminded of a recent research study that discovered, based on reciprocity, we have far few friends than we think we do. In fact, about half as many, if you define a friend as the kind of person who foregoes their Saturday plans to help you move, in the rain, because they know you would do the same for them. That might be a high standard for some people to meet. What is it for a customer to love you as much as you claim they do?

**How do you know your customers love you?** Because they keep giving you money? It would be sad if that were your only metric. Bear in mind, 80% of the companies in the market claim they deliver superior customer service, while only 8% of consumers think those same companies actually do deliver superior customer service.

**A client who does repeat business with you is not a strong indication of love.** Some frequent users actively dislike doing business with you but don't say a word; they just continue to seethe in silence. Only about 4% will share their dissatisfaction with you. So why do they keep coming back? Because they love you? No. Because the switching cost is too high, there's no other viable alternative — yet, or you just aren't a big enough priority in their decision making. The brutal fact is, it is very unlikely all of your customers love you. The good news is, they do not all have to for you to still have strong and reputable customer satisfaction.

**Proper customer service involves an ecosystem** built on your reliability, responsiveness, and your commitment to the relationship. Like any relationship you value, it requires proactive effort, cultivation, and your vigilant attention.

**So how well are you truly doing?** Below are a series of thought-starters, each with a follow up "prove it" question. Use this as an accountability guide for how committed you are to customer service. Don't cheat yourself or your clients, answer honestly.

**1. Is your organization focused on customer service improvement?**
*What was the last thing you improved?*

**2. Does your company have a formal process for improving customer service?** *Where is it documented and who has access to it?*

**3. Does your organization inspect customer service processes?** *How do you know it works?*

**4. Is your organization's vision of ideal customer service clearly defined?** *What is it?*

**5. Has your organization calculated the cost of losing a client?** *How much are they worth?*

**6. Are the employees in your organization clear about who their internal and external customers are?** *Do they serve them differently?*

**7. Does your organization measure customer satisfaction?** *How?*

**8. Are customer facing employees free to take action to resolve a negative customer experience?** *How much authority do they have and do they know it?*

**9. What strategies does your organization use to improve customer satisfaction?** *Name them.*

**10. Does your organization engage in regular training to improve customer service?** *What was the last one? When is the next one scheduled?*

**11. What are the current vital few customer improvement issues your organization must address?** *Knowing what you now know, what is your most important next action?*

Don't be arrogant about customer service. Even if you are doing a fantastic job, it doesn't sell well to brag. You are probably overestimating and likely to set up unfulfillable expectations to new prospects. As an entrepreneur, executive or another leader, use the questions above to improve your customer service.

## *Cultivating Success*

Last week I had a delightful discussion with a colleague about our individual writing processes. As we talked between sips of coffee, it became clear that we had a mutual tendency to make things more complex than they have to be. I hastily narrowed my suggested process down to a five-phase plan.

Capture it.
Write it.
Edit it.
Polish it.
Publish it.

**Capture it** – Have a way of capturing your ideas. Carry a notebook you feel good about scribbling in when a flash of brilliance shines before you. Jot down key words or phrases, make a rough outline or a mind map. Anything to not let the little morsels escape back into the ether.

**Write it** – Set up a time and give yourself permission to write a horrible first draft. You have to get something down in a relatively cogent fashion, but don't censor yourself. Get your first blush of an idea onto the page or screen. Now it's real. You have something to work with. Until you have something, you have nothing.

**Edit it** – Edit what you have. Many people get hung up here. They share their early draft with a group of friends, or strangers in a workshop, pre-apologizing for the purist draft of their heart on the page. Then these, often well-meaning but seldom useful advisors, bleed all over your work with contradictory instructions. The result falls somewhere between a piece written by committee with all the soul burned out of it, or you rocking in a corner, questioning your skills as a writer and your choices in life. Let up on yourself. Find the nuggets you like, and either rewrite your work for better clarity, or shelf it and try again. No big deal. Breathe easy.

**Polish it** – I like to give my writing a chance to breathe. Sometimes I feel like my ideas need a gestational period on the page before further committing to them publicly. However, I do not always have that luxury, and more accurately, the patience. When it is time to polish your writing, go after the grammatical errors and make choices as to whether you will ignore the stringent rules or not. Sometimes you have to live dangerously. Read the piece aloud and make sure you believe it will resonate with your intended audience.

**Publish it** – This next step can be the difficult, scary, and fraught with uncertainty. You need to publish it, or post it or submit it. Wherever you intend it to be read, you need to send your piece there, and then you need to let go. It is now out of your hands. You have done what you could, and you are relatively confident it was enough.

I am convinced if you keep to these steps you will become a better, more prolific and confident writer.

As I reflected on the earlier coffee meeting it dawned on me, there were a similar corresponding set of steps required to cultivate virtually everything. Whether it be growing crops, relationships, business ventures, career management, or leading change, there are five common actions required for success.

**1. Till the Soil** – You have to prepare the field in the most beneficial way possible for what you want to grow. New parents know this as nesting. It is the mental and physical prep work that has to occur, to lay the groundwork, usually before anyone else even notices.

**2. Plant the Seed** – The seed may be something concrete, but in your world, it is more likely an idea, notion, or initiative. Regardless, it has to take root. Otherwise, you've got nothing.

**3. Feed and Weed** – You have to nurture the item or idea you are cultivating. You give it the care and attention it requires, and you remove all the things that could choke it off, compete for its survival, or otherwise inhibit its growth.

**4. Harvest** – Eventually, seldom as soon as you would like but often faster than you would expect, you have to reap what you have sown. Success in this step is about timing and the right resources. Picking things that are still under ripe might be okay in some instances. Leaving what you have grown to languish and rot on the vine is not.

**5. Bring to Market** – Whatever market means to you; it's show time. This is when you share, sell, tell, or perform in front of your intended audience. You will get a reaction, and hopefully profitable praise for your work. Either way, use all the feedback you get to repeat or improve your process.

Each of these five steps calls on you to exert effort. However, there's only so much you can do, before you have to rely on nature, or faith, or God, or science, or some other force that is beyond your current control. You'll notice what happens in the period between each of your actions is out of your hands. This is where the growth occurs.

Sometimes the result will be unexpected, and you will have to make adjustments to get back on track or adapt to the outcome. It is important to recognize, those quiet spaces between the efforts you exhibit is where you have to allow the magic to happen. You can influence these periods, but you cannot control them, and that is what makes the whole thing exhilarating.

## *Friends*

Ever come across a friend or family member who was screwing up their leadership? It usually happens about 18 months into their role. By that time the honeymoon is over and they start clashing with employees and colleagues.

You might not notice it at first. They stopped talking about work as much lately, but something happened and they need to vent.

You listen as they complain about how people have become incompetent, aren't taking direction, and seem to have become stupid overnight. You know, it's *possible* those things may be true, and you want to be supportive, but ... it sure does sound like they're whining.

They are likely under pressure, questioning themselves, feeling a lot of uncertainty, but are trying to hide it behind bravado. That's the wrong tactic and if they proceed, they risk becoming a lousy leader.

Friends don't let friends become lousy leaders. You've got an opportunity to talk some sense into them. Don't squander the trust. Show them some tough love and encouragement.

## *Integrity*

You have no control over your reputation; that's on other people and their opinion of you, which is largely irrelevant. Unless your ego is inflated, and you require outside adulation to find meaning.

You have complete control over your character; forged via your consistent decisions and actions over time.

If you have weak character, you will be susceptible to a wide range of assaults on your reputation. Justified or not, the accusations will stick or linger.

If you have strong character, your reputation becomes unimpeachable because of your integrity.

Decide what kind of person you want to be, and then make decisions and take actions that support that image.

## Find a Way to Laugh

No matter what you are going through, find a way to laugh. There will always be things out of your control. You will experience confusion, anger, hurt, concern, and other emotions you may have never thought possible. That's life. Some days, everything is going your way. Other days, you cannot catch a break.

It's okay.

Like the weather in Boston, wait a minute and conditions will change. Take yourself lightly. Count your gratitudes, then count them again because you undoubtedly missed a few. See clearly, do what you can, endure what you must, and laugh often.

Remember, lessons with laughter last longer.

## *Lousy Leaders Piss Me Off*

Somewhere around 60% of managers fail within two years of taking on the role. There's lots of reasons; from lack of good training and support, or poor hire decisions, to ignorance that management and leadership can be a little thankless and a lot of work. Still, regardless of the burn rate, some ill-intentioned or woefully ignorant people find ways to hang on and corrupt the pool that contains truly exceptional leaders.

There are many contributing factors that go into creating either an excellent or lackluster leader. To be clear, one person's lousy leader could be another's white knight, if perception were the only metric. Thankfully, it's not. Moral leadership has some variance, as does situational awareness, curiosity, stewardship, empathy, and information sharing; but taken together, they paint a clear picture of a leader's capacity.

Ultimately, ideal leadership is based on the current environment, the needs of the times, and the consensus of others. Those variables can change. Lousy leaders seldom adapt.

There really is no excuse for allowing crappy leaders to prevail. Admittedly, I have a visceral reaction to poor leaders, which is why part of my mission is to challenge, disrupt, and dismantle the practice of lousy leadership. By showing others how to mitigate the influence of poor leaders on their lives while building self-confidence and support to expand their own potential, we are making a positive difference.

## *Good Leaders*

Good leaders didn't get that way instantly. They learned and continue to work on themselves. Whether they are starting their own venture, or looking for ways to improve their performance for their team and organization, they seek to be challenged.

Wise ones know they benefit from external accountability. They need someone to act as a sounding board for their ideas.

Even great leaders get drained and need a shot of inspiration and direction to regain their focus to stay or get back on track.

With a constantly changing landscape, it's easy for leaders to feel like they are losing their footing, so the validation and support of others helps to restore their confidence.

## *Art and Science*

One day you started a small business. You've survived hundreds of triumphs and tragedies and suddenly you found yourself responsible for leading others. That's great!

Here's the thing, are you any good at it? Do you know what you're doing, or are you still "faking it until you make it?" You don't really want to play with other people's careers based on whim, do you? Are you consumed with imposter syndrome, or are you brave enough to be vulnerable and build trust?

Leadership combines art and science. There is uniqueness, and there are predictable outcomes. Do you know the difference? No one wants to work with a lousy leader, especially your team.

## *Change Things*

Change things.

Not because you're bored or you think the current way is too difficult for you to achieve.

Change things that are broken, that are causing mayhem, pain and suffering.

Let emotion propel you, not defeat you.

You can be better than this.
We can do better than this.

## *Small Steps*

Do not defer your dreams for so long that they become unrecognizable.

You don't have to make grand gestures in their direction, merely a small, seemingly insignificant step toward it every single day.

## *Mother's Day*

Want to find a leader who is focused on their purpose, inspires action, knows their why, how, what, who, and when; understands servant leadership, praises progress and stays on track against many odds despite minimal recognition?

Look toward the mothers of the world.

Not all of them. Let's not sugar coat it, some aren't up for the role. However, the vast majority are great leaders. Spend some time with them and learn.

Today would be a good day to start.

## *Every Day is Beautiful*

Even when you feel like everything sucks there can be beautiful things waiting for you.

Leadership isn't always easy. Neither is parenting, being a good friend, romance, and many other parts of life. Sometimes things feel effortless, other days arduous. Maybe those days turn into weeks or months. We all go through good periods and bad periods. It's cyclical. It's how it all works. But there is zero excuse for not feeling gratitude every single day. Even when things don't go the way you would prefer, there is magic, and light, and learning in every instant of the day and with every interaction.

So even when things suck, you've got to admit, they don't suck that bad. And when you begin to feel and show appreciation for everything ... even the things that suck ... it's hard to stay pathetic and sad.

**Never deny your emotions. Never deny your dreams. Every day is beautiful, no matter how bleak it seems.**

## *Pricey Mission*

You know what would be stupid?

Spending thousands of dollars on a retreat and getting in arguments over the "best" adjectives; designing, printing, framing, and hanging your company vision, mission, and values on the wall behind the receptionist and no one in the organization being able to tell you what they're working toward.

Ladies and gentlemen this is your competition. From Fortune 500 companies to small businesses in your neighborhood. Lousy leaders invest inordinate time, treasure, and talent to finely craft their company vision, mission, and values and very little on implementing them.

They reveal the results amidst great fanfare, gesticulation, and exclamations of how hard they've worked to achieve these inarticulate, nonsensical, Frankenstein assembled documents. Employees tilt their heads like curious dogs, trying to make sense of what has just amounted to a very expense box to check.

Ask three random employees what the company vision, mission, and values are, and you will learn all you need to know about the organization's leadership. Employees who know or get it approximately right are engaged, inspired, and regularly developing themselves. Those who return the confused puppy face look, have leaders who are disengaged, uninspired, and unimaginative. You don't have to pay a consultant thousands of dollars to figure this out.

Every company has a vision, mission, and values, but very few match those they mount to the wall. What they publicly proclaim is what they aspire too, or believe makes them look good. How they currently act, what they reward, when they administer consequences, and how they treat each other is who they truly are.

## *Be a Leader. Not a Prig. Not a Prick.*

You're there for others. Be a good steward of their trust and faith in you and your vision.

Teach, but more importantly, learn. Always improve.

Do not passively watch. Participate. You do not have to do grand things every day, merely make a difference to those around you. Practice and encourage small acts of courage.

Do not bloviate or announce your ambitions. Instead, work on them. Do not bemoan your shortcomings; lessen them.

Celebrate twice as often as you complain.

It is not about you. It's about others.

Go make a positive difference.

## *Decide to Lead*

First, you have to decide to lead.

Then, you have to decide if you're going to be a Builder, or a Fixer.

A Builder has a vision of something new, an innovation, and is growth-oriented.

A Fixer takes something good and makes it great. They too may innovate and grow, but they're not starting from scratch.

Yes, you can do both, but don't. You'll dilute your efforts. Share your leadership.

When YOU decide to lead, will you be a Builder or a Fixer?

## *Step it Up*

Almost without fail, people I talk with can easily express the attributes of a good leader - often with a spark of admiration and relief.

When they speak of a lousy leader, they become tense, sometimes angry, sometimes withdrawn.

The problem with lousy leaders is, they have no idea they're lousy. I blame "good" leaders for that. There are plenty of people who can correct the corrosive behaviors or poor leadership, but they lack the confidence to stand up.

Lousy leaders can bring down the average far quicker than exceptional leaders can raise it. All the more reason for good leaders to flex their muscles, become comfortable with confrontation and have enough personal power and leverage to not allow themselves to be manipulated by others.

## *Crisis Promotion*

A lot of people like to showboat and brag about how they solved a crisis-level problem. Sometimes they deserve accolades, less for their skill and more for their luck. When you reach a crisis stage it means there have been prior failures of leadership. Procrastination is a big culprit, so is cynical sabotage. People don't get promoted because things go smoothly. They get promoted because they solved a crisis. Start asking where the crisis started and you'll see an absence of leadership.

So maybe, get out of the habit of promoting that person until they get their act together.

## *Roaring Isn't What Makes You a Leader*

It's common to confuse dramatic displays of power for leadership. Theatrics alone result in a limited and short-run performance. Effective leaders know when to roar and when to whisper.

## *Words Matter*

Words matter and sometimes the best word to use is shocking or taboo. Good leaders use restraint and save the swears and slang for high-impact situations. To do otherwise cheapens the effect and your seriousness.

Spare me the arguments of authenticity and being true to yourself.

Grow up.

Language has thousands of adjectives, verbs, and nouns that can easily enhance your message. Relying on a few go-to words or phrases is lazy, whether they are swears or not. Stop deluding yourself into thinking you're edgy when actually, you're a mess. People either tune you out or wince around you because your word choices sound like a fork scraped along a plate. Either way, your message isn't getting heard. Raise your game.

## *Where You Dwell*

It's okay to occasionally talk about your accomplishments and to share stories of the challenges you've faced. It's a way of passing along your knowledge and wisdom to others.

Strong leaders, however don't dwell. They don't seek sympathy or adulation for their work. They work, and their results speak volumes. They don't tell you they are busy, slammed, or buried, because they are professionals, not whiney jack holes.

While it's tempting (and easy) to dwell on what it would be like to be the person you WANT to become someday. It's a better use of your time to know all about the person you currently ARE. Then, double-down on investing in that person. You've already got everything you need to get you where you want to go, but you may have to dig deep to uncover the clues. They're there. Waiting for you.

## *The Myth of Ease*

It is not easy to possess courage when your nerves shake your entire body.

It is not easy to demand accountability, results, and forward movement, when comfort and contentment sets in.

It is not easy to detach from your ego when it demands near constant attention.

It is not easy to ignore your irrational fears when your imagination vividly feeds them.

It is not easy to regularly increase your knowledge and flexibility when you feel certainty and confidence in your ways.

It is not easy to expand rather than contract when you sense scarcity.

It is not easy to embrace dichotomy when you have a clear preference for one over the other.

You do not lead because it is easy. You lead because you must. You lead well, because you care about your integrity, your character, the cause, and the people who freely follow you.

From afar, leadership can look easy. It is a myth. Those who lead poorly dwell on the burdens. Those who lead well, often make it look effortless. Excellent practitioners of any craft, make it look easy to the casual observer. However, they do not concern themselves with the opinion of the casual observer. High performers in any discipline practice in the arena long before spectators arrive.

## *Better Goals*

Imagine how much more we could accomplish if leadership were less of an ego trip or a popularity contest.

What if the number or size of problems solved, crisis averted, lives saved, elders respected and cared for, children fed and educated, defined success instead of the subjective smiley faces on a survey or the number of zeros on a balance sheet?

What if everyone, regardless of condition, stage, or station in life was inspired to adopt projects that used the best of his or her strengths and abilities to contribute to improving a small part of the globe?

What could you fix, enhance, eradicate or disrupt to transform your world?

## *Use Your Voice*

Leaders don't get walked over. They don't always win. They don't always get what they want, but they always tell you what they want. They have enough humility and confidence to rebound off obstacles. They know when to persist and when to move on to something else. They do not brood over every outcome.

Not everyone acts this way. Many suffer in silence. They don't have the confidence to speak nor the support to feel heard. They put others before themselves so often that their preferences become invisible. The devotion can be admirable but not at the expense of self-expression.

Start practicing your leadership. Choose things. You have preferences; begin to identify what they are. Then, when it's important to you, tell others. Give yourself your voice back. People may not hear you. You may fail many times. No one enjoys failing. Leaders don't like failing either, but they don't fear it. They keep going. So should you, because you're becoming a better leader.

Sometimes to preserve the peace or avoid an argument, you adopt the, "go along to get along," attitude. If you're a natural pacemaker, or are accommodating because you don't care, and either outcome is fine, this advice isn't for you. This is for people who want to become better leaders.

You have a voice. Use it. You have a preference. Choose it. Your wants and needs are not less valuable than someone else's. This doesn't absolve you from compromise. You won't always get what you want, but you should start expressing your desires earlier. Doing so let's you and others know where you stand. Quality people will keep your wants in mind in the future. Knowing your preferences help you to know yourself better and get efficient with decision making so you can build the kind of life you want to live.

## *Listen*

Lousy leaders don't listen. It's obvious to everyone but them. Listening isn't just about hearing the words spoken to you. It's paying attention to the person speaking. It's making note of their tone, pace, choice of words, their body language, posture and perspective that influences what they are saying. It's a lot to take in and a lousy leader scoffs, they don't have time for all that. Which is why they are a lousy leader.

Effective leaders invest the time to pick up on and learn these skills, because it helps them communicate. They invest the time in you because they care. They want to get it right. They gather the facts, needs, and concerns that are rational and irrational alike. Yes, it's time consuming at first, but don't you prefer being with people who are as invested in you and your success as they are their own? Isn't that a better interaction than with people who are transactional and take advantage of you?

Shouldn't you start with you? Stop second guessing yourself. Pay attention to your feelings, your body, your mind when things don't seem to add up. Explore, discover, and be curious and kind to yourself and with fellow human beings. You will be amazed at what you can create.

## *Indifference Does Not Influence*

Good leadership involves navigating seemingly opposing ideas to reach truth and consensus. Example, a good leader will not enter into an argument with preconceived notions that they are right. They enter with curiosity to understand other points of view. This allows them time to grow empathy and to alter or strengthen their position. Once they determine the outcome that will be mutually beneficial, they fight for it unreserved fervor.

Ambivalence, indifference, and prolonged detachment does not inspire nor positively influence others. Constantly refine, simplify, and clarify your point of view. Do not deny, hide, or be disingenuous to it.

## *Raise Your Expectations*

Never want to be disappointed? Have low expectations. You exert minimal effort and plod through life. You don't expect much, you don't get much. It's a cynical philosophy way too many people adopt, because it's easier. It's also crappy advice lousy leaders cling on to.

Great leaders know one of life's biggest disappointments is unfulfilled potential. They know that the only way you lift yourself and others is to expand your expectations. People who expect the best often receive the best. Do people fall short? Of course, and good leaders accept the blame and help lift them up.

You can promise good and deliver great all you want. It's a reasonable strategy. But don't ever expect less of people to save yourself disappointment. It's demeaning. Besides, you'll notice the people who adopt this philosophy are typically sullen and angry with the world. They play victim or dole out self-righteous rhetoric. You're better than that.

Effective leaders face disappointments every day. Like everyone else, they would prefer not to be unhappy with results, but they accept reality. Disappointment doesn't debilitate them, it inspires new approaches. They know dwelling in dissatisfaction helps no one.

When you set goals for yourself and others, always raise your expectations. To do otherwise is leadership malfeasance. But don't, "set it and forget it." Help people reach and exceed expectations.

Always.

## *If You Cannot Listen, You Cannot Lead*

You would be amazed at what you can learn when you close your mouth and listen.

When you admit you don't have all of the answers you are open to other solutions.

By letting people fill the silence with their own ideas and thoughts you allow them to reveal underlying concerns. When you know their concerns, dreams and desires, you increase your empathy, greatly improve your negotiation, and inevitably build warmer rapport.

When people feel heard and understood they like you. When they don't, they grow frustrated.

People without good listening skills, personally or professionally, unintentionally broadcast their lousy leadership ability.

The best leaders are the best listeners.

Did you hear that?

## *Your Values Drive Your Behavior*

Your values drive your behavior.
Your behavior demonstrates your values.
When they mismatch each other, you are not being your authentic self.
Many people spend their lives this way because they didn't know they had a choice.
You always have a choice.
You can change your behaviors to match your values.
You can change your values to match your behaviors.
It's better to pick values that are meaningful to you. If you go the other way you will still feel unfulfilled.
Lousy leaders tend to betray their values.
Excellent leaders live their values.
When your values and behaviors are aligned and agree, things work out for you. Your smile returns, your purpose is clear and your days are productive and meaningful

## *Under Appreciating*

Encouragement and appreciation aren't difficult things for good leaders to express. They do it regularly, freely, genuinely, and without expectation. These are things lousy leaders cannot do.

A lousy leader doesn't think to thank you for doing your job. They think you should thank them for giving you the privilege of work.

On the rare occasion they show appreciation, it is either because you have enhanced their riches or status beyond what they imagined you could do; or they are trying to placate you. They received feedback from someone, (maybe you) that they need to be more considerate.

Anyone can fake praise from time to time. Lousy leaders, those who bother to think about it, use praise as a psychological tool to keep you captive. They toss a few crumbs of appreciation every few weeks when it looks like you might cause trouble for them. And, because you are starving, you gobble it up. This intermittent reinforcement keeps you hooked, and you convince yourself that things aren't so bad.

Lousy leaders are insidious to morale and mental health. They warp reality and distort facts to make you second-guess yourself. We have all fallen prey to a lousy leader at some point in our lives and can recognize them and their tactics. That doesn't make it easier for us, particularly if over time, we have grown our affection toward the lousy leader. It is a kind of Stockholm syndrome, and we think it's love. It's not. It's survival.

Make the practice of genuine praise a part of your day. Show gratitude and appreciation the way effective leaders do. It's almost as familiar as breathing. They say thank you in 101 different ways. They notice, listen, and involve you in decisions. They seek your insight and contributions. They don't always act on what you recommend, and they sometimes disappoint you, but they always consider you. And that makes all the difference.

# BONUS - 20 MAXIMS

The following are a collection of maxims and reflections that didn't easily fit into other parts of this book, but I wanted to ensure they were included.

## MAXIM 1
Here's a free leadership tip that if actively pursued each day, will save you lots of money and stress.
Work at being less mean, stupid, or annoying.
Too many people think they can't afford investing in leadership development. If you want to manage better and lead well, you have to; but you don't always have to use money.

## MAXIM 2
Remember, leadership is better when it serves others, not self. Yes, the vision is yours. The direction is yours. But getting there is up to those who follow you.

## MAXIM 3
Effective leaders illuminate. It's not always the fastest, easiest or most effective route, but they avoid lugubrious shadows. They don't need to protect their ego in the darkness. They embrace and correct their faults under the sometimes harsh and disinfecting light.

## MAXIM 4
Have a system to capture all of your ideas. Keep a notebook and jot down 10 or 20 that come to you each morning. You'll find you have no shortage. Some will seem foolish or impractical, but some will put a sparkle in your eye. Act on those ones. Immediately.

## MAXIM 5
Diversity is a strategic advantage. You want a team with differing backgrounds, varied thoughts, experiences, opinions, and expertise. When everyone agrees (or pretends to agree) you are open to exposure and error. You limit growth and the capacity to improve; which is not effective

leadership.

Yes, we should know by now that everyone has their own private demons and struggles. To recognize such, is empathy.
Now, understand that those who face each day despite their challenges have an inner strength and humility. To recognize that, is leadership.

## MAXIM 6
You don't have to LOVE all of the work. You won't ever -- but you had better LIKE it at least 51% of the time. If you don't, start finding ways to change -- either your approach, or the work itself.

## MAXIM 7
Ideas are cheap. Decisions are often rushed and second guessed. Actions make the difference.
Dream. Decide. Do.

## MAXIM 8
It is impossible to not make a difference. You're a human being. You're already making a difference. Now, be deliberate about it. Are you going to make a positive or negative difference? That choice is within your control. Always.

## MAXIM 9
Sure, it's nice to have people sing your praises, but if you insist on it, or EVERYONE on your team participates, you're not leading and some of them are lying.

We're all susceptible to a little ego stroking. Good leaders eschew the applause or share it with others. Lousy leaders devour it as their life force, like vampires to blood.

## MAXIM 10
Don't get too worked up about not having it all figured out yet. Remember, worrying about your purpose is a luxury. It means you're not in survival mood and have time to ponder. Show some gratitude for that fact alone and help other people. That's where you germinate ideas. Your purpose will bloom from there.

## MAXIM 11

You don't always have to be right. You don't have to win every argument or participate in every discussion. To be clear, sometimes you must. When your values and purpose are challenged, do not become complacent. Fight for what you believe in. But preserve your energy for battles worthy of your effort. Do not be goaded into action. Choose kindness. Choose peace. In fact, go out of your way to make peace.

Lay the groundwork for the success you want. Don't be caught off guard. Prepare to receive it. Expect it, not like a spoiled child, but like a farmer tending her crops. You know what you planted. You've nurtured the soil without proof of progress. Soon, vulnerable sprouts appear like fresh ideas. A few will fall to fate, but many will provide the abundance you expected, and often far greater.

You don't know everything. You're not expected to know everything. You are expected to ask. The person asking the questions is the one learning and leading.

## MAXIM 12

Get to know your values and make sure you get along. When there's misalignment, there's trouble.

## MAXIM 13

A lot of managers are frustrated with the performance of their team, so they throw money at the problem and send them off to a leadership retreat or the latest self-discovery training. It doesn't occur to them that they could save time and money by working on themselves first. Instead they create false hope that someone else will fix their problem. Their team may very well improve, but if the leader doesn't, than those changes will be short-lived. When you exempt yourself from learning, growing, and challenging perspectives, you exempt yourself from leadership.

## MAXIM 14

Commitment and competence go hand in hand. It's the foundation of Situational Leadership.

High commitment and high competence will get you great results.

Commitment alone won't get you there. High commitment and low competence is short-lived enthusiasm.

The difference is leadership. Effective leadership bridges the gaps in commitment while developing competence, be it in yourself or others.

Look at results over the long-term, you'll have a good sense of what kind of commitment and leadership it took to achieve those results.

## MAXIM 15
Words make a difference. They can make your heart skip a beat. Others can bring you to your feet. Leaders weave both together. They engage your head and heart.

## MAXIM 16
You can achieve your goal many different ways. It doesn't have to unfold exactly as you planned. Chances are it won't any way. Life uses an outline, not a script.

Pick a direction and head in approximately that direction. There will be obstacles and distractions; some pleasant and others unpleasant. Most interruptions will be unexpected and some will change your life. Fight them, accept them, ignore them, or roll with them. Your choice. Keep heading in the direction of your dreams.

## MAXIM 17
A day without laughter is a day full of wasted opportunities. Yes, there are serious challenges and you may not always feel up to the task. Whine briefly to yourself or an ally who has empathy but no time for pity. Find humor and regain your strength. Lousy leaders lament. Strong leaders laugh.

## MAXIM 18
Lousy leaders can systematically erode the optimistic possibilities held by others. With their influence they are, through ignorance more than intent, creating a new generation of lousy leaders, a cycle that must stop.

## MAXIM 19

If you find yourself dwelling - stop and take action. If you find yourself fretting over things you don't know - go fact-finding. Imagination can create love or hate without uttering a word. Imagination can be beautiful or dangerous. Or both! To make it tangible, you need to take action.

## MAXIM 20

Sometimes all it takes to lift your mood is a smiling baby or a cute furry animal. Nothing wrong with that. We all need a pick me up from time to time ... but don't rely on external motivation. As a leader, you've got to supply internal inspiration. That inspiration comes from confidence and clear intentions. And yes, your confidence and clear intentions come from your internal inspiration. It's a virtuous cycle.

## *Final Thoughts*

Leadership uses the head, heart, and hands.
You need emotion and empathy.
You need intellectual curiosity and reason.
You need the capacity to take action.

Don't overvalue emotion so much that it clouds your judgment. Likewise, avoid over analyzing things you have no control over.

When you find yourself over thinking it's a symptom that you're fearful of doing.

A leader can have fear, but their fear shouldn't stop them. They take the risk. They risk looking vulnerable or inept because they have confidence that if they fail they will recover. They also know that their bias for action more often than not, makes them look strong and knowledgeable.

If you're THINKING too much you're not DOING enough.
Do more.
Get busy.
Take action.

# ABOUT THE AUTHOR

Karl Bimshas, Boston-bred and California-chilled leadership consultant and author of several books and programs designed for busy professionals who want to manage better and lead well.

With an M.S. in Executive Leadership from the University of San Diego and a B.A. in Mass Communications from Emerson College in Boston, Karl Bimshas has held operational and sales leadership positions in public and private corporations. As a sought-after executive coach and leadership consultant, he's helped busy professionals find, set and get their great goals by discovering the a-ha within.

## Want help managing better and leading well in your organization?

Karl Bimshas Consulting is the leadership development and accountability firm that busy professionals turn to help grow their confidence and support around management and leadership.

Visit www.KarlBimshasConsulting.com or call 619-497-2670.

www.ingramcontent.com/pod-product-compliance
Lightning Source LLC
Chambersburg PA
CBHW071025240526
45469CB00006BD/2095